WHAT IS TO BE DONE?

WHAT IS TO BE DONE?

A play by

MAVIS GALLANT

With an introduction by Linda Leith

What Is To Be Done? was first published in 1983 by Quadrant Editions.
Reissued 2017 by Linda Leith Publishing.
What Is To Be Done? © 2017 The Estate of Mavis Gallant.
Introduction © 2017 Linda Leith.

All rights reserved. No part of this book may be reproduced for any reason or by any means without permission in writing from the publisher.

Names, characters, places, and incidents are either the product of the author's imagination or are used fictitiously, and any resemblance to actual persons, living or dead, businesses, companies, events, or locales is entirely coincidental.

Cover design: Salamander Hill Design
Book design: WildElement.ca
Printed and bound in Canada.

Library and Archives Canada Cataloguing in Publication

Gallant, Mavis, 1922-, author
    What is to be done? / Mavis Gallant.

A play.
Issued in print and electronic formats.
ISBN 978-1-988130-22-4 (softcover).--ISBN 978-1-988130-23-1 (EPUB).--
ISBN 978-1-988130-24-8 (Kindle). ISBN 978-1-988130-25-5 (PDF)

    I. Title.
PS8513.A593W53 2017   C812>.54   C2017-902044-7
                                                     C2017-902045-5

The publisher gratefully acknowledges the support of the Canada Book Fund, of the Canada Council for the Arts, and of Société de développement des entreprises culturelles, SODEC.

Linda Leith Publishing
Montreal
www.lindaleith.com

CONTENTS

Montreal in Wartime
Introduction by Linda Leith   7

What Is To Be Done?
A play by Mavis Gallant   25

MONTREAL IN WARTIME
AN INTRODUCTION TO
MAVIS GALLANT'S *WHAT IS TO BE DONE?*

Mavis Gallant's play *What Is To Be Done?* opens in August 1942 and closes on May 8th, 1945, VE Day. Its setting is Montreal, and its subject, like that of the revolutionary pamphlet by Vladimir Ilyich Lenin from which it takes its title,[1] is the dream of a better world.

The two young women who are the main characters in the play—Jenny Thurstone, aged 18, and Molly McCormack, 20—may be the most engaging characters Gallant ever created, the most hopeful, and also the most naïve. When the play opens, they are socialist activists receiving instruction from an older woman, Mrs. Bailey, and from a young man from Glasgow named Willie Howe.

Lenin's dream was of socialist revolution; the young women's dream is of the new world that will emerge when the war ends. As Jenny tells Molly, it will be "a clean new world, with a clean swept sky" (55).[2]

Mavis Gallant, who was born Mavis de Trafford Young in

---

1   V. I. Lenin, *What Is To Be Done? Burning Questions of Our Movement*. Marxist Internet Archive, 1969.

2   Page numbers in this introduction refer to the play unless otherwise identified.

Montreal in 1922 and died in Paris in 2014, is celebrated internationally as a writer of short stories, over a hundred of which were first published in *The New Yorker,* as well as of two novels and numerous essays. The British director Clifford Williams expressed interest in a play and, when that did not result in a production in England, she sent the manuscript of *What Is To Be Done?* to the Canadian director John Hirsh at Stratford. He passed it on to the Tarragon Theatre in Toronto[3] and, in early 1982, she received a telegram from artistic director Urjo Kareda who then followed up with a letter on March 15, 1982: "I love *What Is To Be Done?* and would like to present it as part of my first season as artistic director of the Tarragon. I was immensely drawn to its vitality and its humour, to its fascinating mixture of irony and compassion; and I am mad about those two women."[4]

The play premiered at Toronto's Tarragon Theatre on Remembrance Day, 1982. Reviewers were struck by the focus on the two young women, with Gina Mallet in *The Globe and Mail* calling the play "a treat" and describing the actors Margot Dionne (Molly) and Donna Goodhand (Jenny) as "enchanting." A second *Globe* piece that same day, by Carole Corbeil, argues that Gallant takes "a very female approach," appropriate for the play's subject. Corbeil sees the play as "a mix of the absurdity of 40s French comedies, evocative naturalism, and off-the-wall surrealism." Like Mallet, she, too, loves the two women, saying that "Miss Goodhand and Miss Dionne give gorgeous performances as two women friends united by conspiracy; this is a rare enough sight in the theatre." *Maclean's* describes the play – "an accomplished theatre debut" – as "ambitious, invigorating and blessed with a quirky rhythm

---

[3] See Martin Knelman's article, "Coming Home," *Saturday Night,* Dec. 1982, 69-70.

[4] Letters are quoted with the permission of the estate of Urjo Kareda.

which continually employs indirection to find direction out."[5]

A later review of the published play praises the play's "perfect writing," Gallant's "fine ear for Canadian dialogue, her observations on Canadian society and her attunement to the Canadian sense of humour" which "places Gallant firmly among the finest English-Canadian writers. *What Is To Be Done?* is a continual delight to its reader." Such criticism as there was of the play focuses on time spent on scene changes and on the fact that much of the conflict is off-stage. Tickets sold briskly throughout the six-week run. In the *Toronto Star*, Sid Adilman wrote that it "sold out the first two weeks, tickets are going fast for this week, its third, and the rest of the run. Extra matinées are scheduled for Dec. 1 and 15." He ended his piece with a complaint that this "hot ticket" must be taken off Dec. 19 after six weeks.[6]

Gallant was in Toronto for rehearsals and for the premiere, and when she returned to Paris, Kareda wrote to her: "How we all miss you! It was so exciting to have you with us. Excitement, however, has not ceased. *What Is To Be Done?* is what must be called a runaway success" (Nov. 19, 1982).

"I'm pleased for them," she noted in her journal, along with her thoughts about the production: "As for me, I had a hard core of confidence under the anxiousness. The whole enterprise seemed charmed from the moment I saw a rehearsal. What I can't bear is

---

5   Gina Mallet, "What Is To Be Done? a treat at Tarragon" and Carole Corbeil, "Gorgeous performances in a wry play," *The Globe and Mail*, Nov. 12, 1982; Mark Czarnecki, "Daughters of revolution," *Maclean's*, Nov. 22, 1982.
6   Patrick O'Neill, review of the published book in *Atlantis*, Vol. 10, No. 2, 1985, 204; Sid Adilman, "What's to be done about Gallant's hit?" *The Star*, Nov. 29, 1982. The play became a 1st Choice television production in 1983, and a Montreal production was mounted at the Centaur Theatre in 1984.

that in four weeks it will cease to exist" (Journal, Nov. 24, 1982).[7]

Kareda wrote again after the last performance, a long, single-spaced letter about the "feelings that passed through me, through so many of us, at the final performance of *What Is To Be Done?*" "The production was like some gorgeous soaring balloon, which spun around in the air-currents and kept reaching higher and higher. The actors were so confident and polished and joyous in their work: what they achieved did seem superhuman. The two girls glowed with such grace and radiance and life that you wanted to hug them every moment... Thank you so much for giving us these women and their world and their hopes" (Dec. 28, 1982).

His letter arrived after the holidays, and Gallant found it "so extraordinary and heart-lifting that I went straight out to [rue] Vaugirard and had it copied. Why? What do I think I am going to do with the copies ... ? I think it was just something that made me happy and wanted the happiness multiplied. He says that it is not 'just another play but that in some way it changed all their lives'" (Journal, Jan. 6, 1983).

★★★

Reading the play reminds us that Gallant's career began in wartime Montreal. She became a published writer when a couple of her short stories appeared in little magazines in the 1940s and, she told an interviewer, was writing voluminously—"I wrote more than I've ever done since, I think; now I'm very slow"—and keeping everything she wrote in a "picnic hamper full of manuscripts. Novels, poems, plays, stories."[8]

Most of what she has let us know about her during this period

---

[7] Excerpts from letters and unpublished journals are quoted with the permission of the estate of Mavis Gallant.

[8] *Canadian Fiction Magazine #28* (1978), 32; henceforth CFM.

comes from occasional interviews and from the introduction to *Home Truths*. Like the play, the Linnet Muir stories were written in the late 1970s and set in Montreal. As Gallant herself said in a *Paris Review* interview, they are "as close to autobiography as fiction can be,"[9] but they are still fiction. Bringing *What Is To Be Done?* back into print will make it possible for Gallant's admirers to consider what the play adds to what we know about the artist as a young woman.

Most of her fiction focuses on the worlds she got to know after she left Montreal for Europe in 1950. Though she writes about Canadian or American characters in many of her European stories, few of these characters appear particularly close to her, and it was only in the mid-1970s that she first focused her attention on the Montreal she knew as a child and then as a young woman. It is not coincidental that the mid-1970s were also a time when she was immersed in work on a non-fiction book about the French Jewish artillery officer Alfred Dreyfus, who had been unjustly convicted of treason in 1894. The Dreyfus book had been commissioned and, as she explains in her introduction to *Home Truths*, Captain Dreyfus was not a character she found greatly appealing. He was, in fact, unlike her in almost every way: "Nothing could be more remote from me than someone who deliberately could choose a life of rules and restrictions, of living by the book – and such a thin volume—with only a soldier's options: 'I obey them' and 'They obey me,' both of which are to me totally abhorrent" (HT xxii).

Her work on Dreyfus, however, is what led to her writing about Montreal. She explains that she used to try to imagine the Paris that Dreyfus knew:

---

9   Mavis Gallant told interviewer Daphne Kalotay that friends who knew her as a young women were struck by the similarity with Linnet Muir, telling her, "That is you. Every gesture, every word, every everything is what you were like." "The Art of Fiction 160," *The Paris Review* No. 153, Winter 1999.

> Gradually, as I restored his Paris, his life, I discovered something in common with that taciturn, reserved military figure: we had both resolved upon a way of life at an early age and had pursued our aims with overwhelming singlemindedness. He had been determined to become an officer in the French army, over his family's advice and objections, just as I had been determined to write as a way of life in the face of an almost unanimous belief that I was foolish, would fail, would be sorry, and would creep back with defeat as a return ticket.

At this point, she found herself able to move with greater sureness into her work on Dreyfus, which she had sometimes thought of "as a river where I was drifting farther and farther from shore."

> At the same time—I suppose about then—there began to be restored in some underground river of the mind a lost Montreal. An image of Sherbrooke Street, at night, with the soft gaslight and leaf shadows on the sidewalk—so far back in childhood that it is more a sensation than a picture—was the starting point. Behind this image was a fictional structure of several stories, three wartime stories, then the rest. (HT xxii)

We don't have the Dreyfus book, which has not been published, but we do have Gallant's recreation of the Montreal of the 1920s and the 1940s in the Linnet Muir stories—and we do have *What Is To Be Done?* In Linnet, in Jenny, and in Molly, we have vivid portraits of young women whose hopes and fears and passions and dreams tell us as much as we may ever know about the young woman who became Mavis Gallant. Jenny especially has much in common with Gallant herself as well as with Linnet Muir. Like Gallant, Linnet has a French-speaking nanny and attended a severe French Catholic boarding school at a tender age. Linnet's father dies when she is ten, and her mother remarries and moves away from Montreal; the same was true of Mavis.

In 1940, at eighteen, Linnet finishes school in New York and returns on her own to Montreal much as Gallant herself had done. Linnet is carrying just a $5 bill, her birth certificate, a small suitcase, and what she describes as an "Edwardian picnic hamper." This hamper is full of the poems and journals that, Linnet says, "I had judged fit to accompany me into my new, unfettered existence." There are a few books in Linnet's hamper, too, including "Zinoviev and Lenin's *Against the Stream*" and "a few beige pamphlets from the Little Lenin Library, purchased second-hand in New York" (HT 220-21). Readers of *What Is To Be Done?* may consider the possibility that *Against the Stream* might not have been the only Lenin publication in the picnic hamper.

Mavis Gallant found work similar to the work that Linnet Muir finds in a Montreal office—and to the clerical work that Jenny Thurstone is doing in the Department of Appraisements and Averages of a Montreal newspaper. Jenny spends much of the play hoping to move out of clerical work into the editorial department of the newspaper called *The Beacon* in the play. Linnet marries a man named Blanchard and becomes a journalist for *The Lantern*. In 1944 Gallant herself, now married to John Gallant, was hired as a reporter by a Montreal newspaper called *The Standard*.

When she decided to leave Montreal, she dug out one of the stories from the picnic hamper, typed it up, and submitted it to *The New Yorker*. The magazine replied that the story was too Canadian for them and asked if she had any others. They accepted the second story she sent them, and it appeared in the magazine in 1951, by which time Gallant was in Europe.

"She [Linnet] isn't *myself*," Gallant wrote in the introduction to her collection, *Home Truths*, "but a kind of summary of some of the things I once was. In real life I was far more violent and much more impulsive and not nearly so reasonable" (HT xxii).[10]

This is an intriguing remark, given that Linnet herself is impulsive and unreasonable, if not exactly violent—she is a well-mannered young woman. Though there is no sign of any kind of violent behaviour in Jenny Thurstone, and not much impulsiveness, the play certainly reveals the depths of her personal rebelliousness and of her political radicalism in ways we never see in Linnet—and ways we might not have imagined of Gallant herself. Jenny is bohemian in her dress, her hair, her casually furnished apartment, and both she and Molly—the Molly of the early scenes, at least—are winsome. Jenny and Molly are coached in Stalinist orthodoxy by Willie and the stalwart Mrs. Bailey, who spends most of the play knitting balaclava helmets for the war effort. The Nazis have invaded the Soviet Union, and Stalin wants the Allies to open up a Second Front in Western Europe in order to draw German forces away from the USSR. For a pair of romantic young socialists like Jenny and Molly, the Second Front becomes a rallying cry. Jenny has been studying Russian, just as Linnet attends Russian evening classes at McGill, "for reasons having mainly to do with what I believed to be the world's political future" (HT 243).

Gallant never, to our knowledge, went into detail about the anti-Fascist views she held so passionately as a young woman. The play soon makes it clear that Jenny and Molly are not Trotskyites,

---

10 Introduction to *Home Truths: Selected Canadian Stories*. Toronto : McClelland & Stewart, 1982; HT in page references to the introduction and the Linnet Muir stories, here published together for the first time.

but doesn't provide much of an idea of what they might actually be. They clearly admire Stalin, but then Stalin was one of the Allies in the war against Fascism. Willie's description of Jenny and Molly as "the natural daughters of Bakunin and Queen Victoria," is a comic allusion to Bakunin-style anarchism that serves mostly to distance the young women from the kind of earnest political seriousness that characterizes Mrs. Bailey. It's a description that also suggests that the young women's devotion to radical politics (and to Queen Victoria) is incomplete. No surprise, therefore, that Jenny never does finish painting the Second Front sign on her living room wall. By the end of the play she has painted it over, so that the unfinished SECOND FRON sign is barely visible.

★★★

Far from being Gallant's only comic work—much of her fiction is richly comic—the play is unique in its delight in the kinds of comedy that prose fiction can only suggest: voice, accent, and costuming, as well as such props as the Second Front sign, the radio, a toaster, the portrait of Stalin, and the doughty Mrs. Bailey's knitting.

For the period covered by the play, Social Democrats, Socialists, Marxists, Anarchists, Communists, and Trotskyites of all persuasions are on the same side as Royalists in the fight against Fascism; God is evidently on the same side, too, at least for some—Molly's mother never goes out except to go to Mass, and Molly herself chooses to keep the word GOD when the GOD BLESS THE RED ARMY sign is broken up at the end of the rally.

The most determined left-wing radical in the play is Mrs. Bailey, who replaces the portrait of her own father with one of Stalin. At the outset, though, Willie and all three of the women are also active supporters of the Soviet Union. When Molly shows

Jenny the tattered copy of Lenin's pamphlet that she inherited from her father, Jenny treats it reverentially.

For most of the period covered by the play, Jenny and Molly are not only idealistic, but also naïve. "We thought almost any foreigner had to be on our side," Molly says when the war is drawing to an end (47). She and Jenny had been so blinded by their romantic view of refugees that they couldn't distinguish between those who were left-wing and those who were themselves Fascists. Unable to see the Austro-Hungarian Friendship Club for what it was—a Fascist hang-out—they resisted recognizing that a friend of Willie's, Karl-Heinz, is the enemy.

Montreal has been filling with refugees in the short stories, too, and they are "a source of infinite wonder" to Linnet Muir. "I could not get enough of them," she says. "They came straight of out the twilit Socialist-literary landscape of my reading and my desires" (HT 261). As a young woman, Linnet sees these wartime refugees as "prophets of a promised social order that was to consist of justice, equality, art, personal relations, courage, generosity." Looking back, though, the older Linnet who is telling these Montreal stories knows that she understood only part of the story:

> That the refugees tended to hate one another seemed no more than a deplorable accident. Nationalist pigheadedness, that chronic, wasting, and apparently incurable disease, was known to me only on Canadian terms and I did not always recognize its symptoms [....] They were the only people I had met until now who believed, as I did, that our victory would prove to be a tidal wave nothing could stop. What I did not know was how many of them hoped and expected their neighbours to be washed away too. (HT 261)

Karl-Heinz's reference, in the play, to spending time in a Moscow jail is what finally convinces Jenny that he must be a Fascist, or perhaps a Trotskyite, although she's never met a Trotskyite, and doesn't "even know what they look like" (47).

★★★

Mavis Gallant adored Montreal in the 1940s. When I interviewed her in 1986 for a book on Montreal writers, she was delighted to have an opportunity to talk about her youth in the city she thought "unique."

> It was unique. It was a wonderful, thrilling time to be young. All the old conservative dead weight was still there, and of course French Canada was still locked, but there were elements breaking out, and that was what was so exciting. I'm thinking of the painters particularly, and in a city that size you tend to all know one another – the bohemia. I wonder if I would have said that of any city, but I don't think so, because you couldn't have said it of Toronto in those days. And there was something thrilling about Montreal: the two languages, the centre still hadn't been destroyed as it is now, and it was full of shade trees and attractive stone houses and the stone houses had been made into little flats for a lot of artists and writers and young people.[11]

---

11   Linda Leith, *Writing in the Time of Nationalism*. Winnipeg: Signature Editions, 2010, 32. Gallant's insistence on the word "unique" may have had some influence on her friend William Weintraub's *City Unique: Montreal Days and Nights in the 1940s and 50s*. Toronto: McClelland & Stewart, 1996.

At nineteen, doing clerical work, Linnet Muir describes herself as being "deeply happy. It was one of the periods of inexplicable grace when every day is a new parcel one unwraps, layer on layer of tissue paper covering bits of crystal, scraps of words in a foreign language, pure white stone. I spent my lunch hours writing in notebooks, which I kept locked in my desk. The men never bothered me, apart from trying to feed me little pieces of cake" (HT 248).

In the play, Jenny Thurstone keeps coming up with story ideas for the newspaper editor, Mr. Gillespie, but there is no indication of her keeping a journal and no mention of a picnic hamper. She does have much else in common with both Linnet and Mavis Gallant herself. In her new apartment, in Scene IV, she is engaged in a hopeless attempt at tidying the room. "She does not walk – she dances. This is not affectation, but pure happiness" (47).

Where Molly is proud of her father's fighting spirit, Jenny is sheepish about her own father's privileged background. "G. E. Thurstone, remittance man" is described in the play as being "seedy, boozy, obtuse, but rather splendid. Defiantly English clothes; that is, to a North American eye in 1942, casual, sloppy, unpressed" (23). He appears on stage briefly in a scene from Jenny's childhood, asking her to "Spell 'ate.' The child spells what she has heard: "E-T" (23).

Linnet Muir, in one of the stories, thinks of a hapless English character named Frank Cairns as a "remittance man." She writes a story of her own about the sad fate of the son of a powerful man who, disappointed in the son for whatever reason, provided him with an income—the remittance—on condition that he stay out of England. She quotes a conversation between one such remittance man and his child:

"A-t-e is *et*, darling, not ate."

"I can't say et. Only farmers say et."

"Perhaps here – but you won't always be here."

Jenny is wistful about her father, thinking he was lonely, thinking about his death: "And he died," she tells Molly. "Oh, not like your father. Not fighting. No, he just gradually vanished. Like an old photograph that's been left in a harsh light." In one of the most poignant moments in the play, she continues:

> He gave me what he could. Within his limits. He gave me books ... and music ... and drawing ... and dancing ... and French ... and riding ...."

Molly's response undercuts the merest hint of sentimentality. "You've had a lot to overcome" (24).

Jenny refers to her stepfather as "a Mr. Herbert" – Molly comments that "you sound as though you scarcely knew him" (24) – and the privilege Jenny has known from her father clearly extends to her mother, who "doesn't understand about my working. She doesn't understand the difference between working for a lark and for a living" (32).

In short, the two young women in *What Is To Be Done?* share so many characteristics with Linnet—and with Gallant—that it is easy to overlook how much further the play goes than the stories in its interest in what it was really like to be a young woman in those war years. We have long known that Gallant has described her wartime self as a "romantic socialist"—convinced, as Linnet Muir is convinced, that "our victory over Fascism would be followed by a sunburst of revolution." One of Linnet's colleagues nicknames her "Bolshie" (HT 252), in part because of her political views. Gallant describes herself as having been an "intensely left-wing political romantic" as a young woman: "passionately anti-Fascist, having believed that a new kind of civilization was going to grow out of the ruins of the war — out of victory over Fascism" (CFM 39).

Dramatic as these revelations may have been to Gallant's readers when she made them in a 1978 interview, they are too insubstantial to allow us to imagine the kind of young woman she must have been. The Montreal stories say more, but always in Linnet's own voice, so that we catch barely a glimpse of her. It is only in the play that we see the young women sitting at the feet of the doctrinaire Mrs. Bailey, follow them into the streets of Montreal for demonstrations, listen to their thoughts, understand their dreams and then their misgivings about the future that awaits them.

Linnet Muir is envious of men and ambivalent, at best, about other women. Men are "born without the obstacles and constraints attendant on women" (HT 238), so that Linnet cannot understand why they settle for such small and disappointing lives. The example of the women in the office is discouraging, and that of young women "parked like third-class immigrants at the far end of the room" is repellent (HT 255). Linnet has so little interest in marriage—and she views married women with such distaste—that it comes as a surprise to us (as it evidently does to her co-workers) when she herself gets married.

Gallant's ambivalence about women has puzzled her readers, who have seldom found the women in her fiction particularly delightful, and who have seldom loved them as much or as enthusiastically as those familiar with the play love Jenny and Molly. Some critics of her fiction question whether Gallant herself loves her women characters. Janice Kulyk Keefer, in an essay that shows no awareness of the play, argues that Gallant is "hard on her heroines" and lacks "compassion for her characters." "Why," she asks, "is Gallant so repeatedly ruthless or at best, indifferent, to her heroines"?[12] It's a fair enough question of some of the fiction, but not one that is ever likely to be asked of *What Is To Be Done?*

For the play shows enormous affection for two young women on the cusp of life. Here, Gallant is anything but indifferent to her heroines, as artistic director Urjo Kareda recognized as soon as he read it. The ambivalence about women that is puzzling in Linnet is still perceptible, but no longer puzzling. The play transforms that one young woman's ambivalence into sympathy by dramatizing the differences between two young women with very different voices. Where Jenny is single and professionally ambitious, with no close family—very like Linnet, very like Gallant herself—Molly is married with a child and in frequent contact with her own mother, who looks after the child—and reviewer Gina Mallet finds both these young women "enchanting" on stage. In this split into two characters Gallant can focus her undivided attention on marriage and family in one breath, and in the next breath can focus her undivided attention on a young woman's desire for a career and a life of her own.

Jenny is the character who has most in common with Gallant and with Linnet. In just one respect, though—her marriage—Molly is closer both to Mavis Gallant, née Young, and to Linnet Blanchard, née Muir. Molly's marriage to Duncan, who is overseas for the duration of the war, gives the play great scope to comment on a young woman's romantic, sexual, marital, domestic, and professional disappointments. In friendship, Molly says, "there are no mortgages," and "no one can claim a right to examine the books," but love is "just one foreclosure after another" (25).

---

12 "Mavis Gallant's World of Women: A Feminist Perspective," *Atlantis*, Vol 10, No. 2, 1985. 11-29.

Anxious about her future with Duncan, she has decided that the only way her marriage can work when he gets back to Montreal is for Molly herself to change into whatever he "imagined he married." She is increasingly troubled as the war draws to an end, saying, "I've got to live with him for something like fifty years." Jenny cannot imagine why anyone would want any such thing (35).

If Gallant regards each of these two women with her whole attention and boundless affection, she does so in full knowledge of the disappointments that lie ahead for them; it is this knowledge that makes the play's comedy so poignant. Molly is aware that she is holding a job for Duncan—is in fact holding his job until he gets back and can take over again. From far away in England, he's interested in her money. "He wants to know how I'm spending my money. Money *I* make." At his request, he comes up with a realistic household budget, which she finds less than inspiring. "My future," she says, studying the budget. "What I'm looking at is my future" (38).

Molly and Jenny have been talking all along about what will happen "after the war." They were certain that the first thing the men will do is "get rid of Franco." By June 1944, however, Molly has taken a different view. Instead of getting rid of Franco, she now thinks, the first thing the men will do is "Get rid of us." Knowing that Duncan will take his job back, she warns Jenny to be careful or she, too, will lose her job: "As for you," she advises sternly, "if you want to keep a foot in the door, stop pestering Mr. Gillespie" (38).

Molly, the one who was afraid of change, is the one who changes, becoming increasingly conventional in her dress and personal style and distancing herself from the radical political views that she and Jenny shared earlier in the war. Rewriting the past to match the future, she no longer talks about getting rid of Franco: "Isn't that what we always said, First thing we do after victory is call Franco" (52). Jenny flings the bundle of balaclava helmets in the air and begins to pull a strand of wool around the furniture. "Be careful," Molly says. "It's unravelling" (52).

Indeed, everything is unravelling, all their hopes and dreams. Jenny has her own share of disappointments. Disappointment at losing Molly, when Molly's mother puts her foot down and puts an end to the friendship. Sexual disappointment, too, in Jenny's relationship with Willie. "I said to him, 'You mean that was it? I said, 'Are you sure there isn't some other thing we can do?'" (55).

At the end of the play, Jenny can scarcely believe the horror and injustice that have survived the war. Thinking he knows what she wants, the evidently well-intentioned Mr. Gillespie offers Jenny "a good future" (57), but the future he has in mind has nothing in common with the better world Jenny had hoped for. All that Mr. Gillespie can offer her at the dawn of this new era is a new retirement plan, a new desk, and a new calculating machine. Nothing even close to a clean new world, with a clean swept sky.

Linda Leith
Montreal, May 2017

WHAT IS TO BE DONE?

A play by

MAVIS GALLANT

CAST

MRS. BAILEY

WILLIE HOWE

JENNY

MOLLY

JENNY'S FATHER, G. E. THURSTONE

MOLLY'S FATHER, MICK M^cCORMACK

BARMAN

KARL-HEINZ

MONTREAL

SCENE I	Willie's room, August 1942.
SCENE II	Willie's street. Same night.
SCENE III	New Year's Eve at the Austro-Hungarian Friendship Club, 1942.
SCENE IV	Jenny's room, Summer 1943.
SCENE V	Second Front Rally, January 1944.
SCENE VI	Jenny's room, June 1944.
SCENE VII	Any room, Summer 1944.
SCENE VIII	Willie's new room, December 1944.
SCENE IX	Jenny's room, 7 May 1945.
SCENE X	Same, 8 May 1945.

SCENE I

August 1942. Willie's room.

RADIO *(Voice emphatic and cheerful)*
… from Vo-RO-nezh … one moment … allow me to correct that, please. From VO-ronezh to the Black Sea …
(Static)
General von … sorry, I'm having a little trouble reading the name. General von has reached the Bock. Let me just take that again. General von Bock has reached the Don.
(Static)
… Prime Minister Winston Churchill is in Moscow for a friendly meeting with …
(Static)
… during which the Russian leader has asked for a military operation …
(Pronouncing with difficulty, as though reading a foreign language)
… an engagement… which he calls … a Second Front…
(Increasingly cheerful)
Today, August 14th, the weather continued to be humid and hot, with temperatures in the high nineties. Offices and stores closed early here in Montreal, a number of persons having collapsed owing to heat prostration. Light casualties were

reported at Danceland Paradise, when the dancefloor caved in.
(Static)
... wishing to draw the extra sugar ration for making jam and pickles should present their ...

(Record of 'Oh Rose Mark, I love you ...'
Stops abruptly, as if put on by mistake.
Record of 'A-Hunting We Will Go.'

During this, Willie Howe's room has been revealed. A window covered with a blanket. A kitchen table on which is an old-fashioned radio, a large tea-cosy, and a bachelor's muddle of cups and glasses. Electric fixture with dangling wires. Bed with suitcase underneath. Spanish War posters. Four plain kitchen chairs.

Molly, Jenny, Willie Howe, Mrs. Bailey.

Molly is 20, Jenny 18, Willie about 27, Mrs. Bailey another generation altogether.

Willie sits between Molly and Jenny. Mrs. Bailey, apart, knits a balaclava helmet as if the war depended on it. The women are dressed for a hot summer night — cotton dresses, bare arms and legs, plain sandals. No makeup or jewelry, though Molly and Mrs. Bailey wear wedding rings. The younger women's hair is long and straight. A fanatical neatness. Molly holds a large paper bag.

Willie is dressed for a Bible Society meeting in a damp chapel: Dark suit, sober tie, clumsy respectable boots. To a North American eye, in 1942, he would seem shabby, provincial and poor.

    MRS. BAILEY   *Turning off 'A-Hunting We Will Go')*
        All right... Willie. Carry on.

WILLIE   *(Strong Glasgow)*
         If you two girls are sincerely interested in politics, remember that the first rule is never to have friends who might be friends of other friends.

JENNY   *(Across Willie to Molly)*
         What do you make of the accent? Is it real?

MOLLY   I'm not sure. Wait till he says something else.

WILLIE   It is a wise rule, in fact, to have no friends at all.

MOLLY   It isn't natural. It's nerves.

Willie bends down and unties his bootlaces. Seems to wonder why he has done this. Tries to tie them again. One breaks.

MOLLY   Foreigners wear ugly shoes.

JENNY   Does he count as foreign? He speaks English. Sort of. He does seem poor. What could make him foreign.

WILLIE   *(Giving up on the bootlaces)*
         No friends at all. A wise rule.

MOLLY   He can't be poor. He's a designer. He made one of those posters.

WILLIE   As for the second wise rule of political action ...

JENNY   What does he do with his money, then?

MOLLY   I think he's being blackmailed. By the Trotskyites in Glasgow.

JENNY   That's terrible.

WILLIE   ... the importance of complete discretion. The doors and windows amply curtained. The telephone muffled and isolated ...

MOLLY   He fought in Spain, you know. They blackmail each other like anything.

Molly offers the bag of biscuits to Mrs. Bailey, who shakes her head, knitting fiercely. Molly offers it to Willie.

MOLLY   *(Quite loudly, as though Willie were bound to be deaf)* Have a ginger biscuit, Willie. Go ahead. Take a handful. We brought them for you.

Willie takes several. Removes crumbs from his chin with a large handkerchief.

MOLLY   *(To Jenny, both eating biscuits)* Not a bad place for an immigrant. I wonder if he found it straight off?

JENNY   The tea-cosy belongs to Mrs. Bailey.

MOLLY   Can you read what it says on the posters?

JENNY   'No pasaran.' It could mean anything.

WILLIE   *(Still having trouble with crumbs)* The third rule of politics is this ... When ... *(He chokes)*

JENNY   That's not a very nice looking handkerchief.

MOLLY   Left-wing foreigners are always snobby about using Kleenex.

JENNY   Just between us, Molly. Is Willie a *real* Stalinist? He seems — I don't know — too confused.

MOLLY   I've been wondering that too.

MRS. BAILEY   *(To Willie)* Try holding your breath. I'll take over. Girls! We're wasting time. What is the Movement?

JENNY   The Movement is a capacious vehicle moving at its own speed.

JENNY   ... from its starting point to its objective ...

MOLLY   Time being in its favour ...

JENNY   We've left something out.

MOLLY   From its starting point to its objective ...

JENNY   No, we went wrong before that. Willie's fainted.

MOLLY   The heat. It must be over a hundred in here. *(Molly starts for the window)*

MRS. BAILEY   You know that we do not open windows.

MOLLY   Nobody can see in — we're on the third floor.

JENNY   Besides, we're not doing anything. Just sitting around eating biscuits.

MRS. BAILEY   You are not just sitting around. You are receiving instruction.

JENNY   *(Wishing to be agreeable)* It *is* something like Confirmation class. What is your name? M or N.

MRS. BAILEY   The immediate need is for ...

JENNY AND MOLLY   A Second Front.

MRS. BAILEY   A real Stalinist knows ...

MOLLY   Some of the answers.

JENNY   Most of the answers.

MOLLY   Where to find the answers.

JENNY   All the questions.

MRS. BAILEY   The first thing we do after the war is ...

JENNY   *(Happily)*
Get rid of Franco.

MOLLY   After the war, the men won't let a Fascist state exist.

JENNY   They'll never put up with it.

MOLLY   They're learning, now. Contact with European workers ...

JENNY   With political unions ...

MRS. BAILEY   What does your husband say, Molly?

MOLLY   Not much. He's in England, and you know how that is. Feudal. Still by the time they all get to Berlin ...

JENNY   They'll have learned not to take things lying down any more. The way they took the Depression.

MRS. BAILEY   Jenny. Jenny. You're preaching counter-revolution.

JENNY   I am?

WILLIE   *(Faintly)*
There is a fourth wise rule ...

MOLLY   *(To Jenny)* You can read Duncan's letter about the situation in England, if you like. It's in the bag, under the biscuits. Don't read the last paragraph. That's only for married people.
(At the window) If Willie doesn't need air, some of the rest of us do. *(Tugs at blanket, which falls)* Jenny, come and look at the stars. *(Jenny engrossed in last paragraph)* I told you not to read that. *(Molly removes the tea-cosy, revealing Willie's telephone)*

MRS. BAILEY   *(To Molly)* Just let me try this for shape.

MOLLY   *(To Mrs. Bailey)* I have to call my mother.

MRS. BAILEY   Your heart's in the right place, Molly, but if you go on like this you'll never be useful.
(Fits balaclava helmet over Molly's head)

JENNY   *(Gently fanning Willie with the letter)* This is a beautiful apartment, Willie. I mean it. I'd give anything to have one like it. But you have to pay black market prices for leases now. I can't save up enough. The reason why I've never joined the Movement is I've never had the two dollars.

MOLLY   *(To Mrs. Bailey, who removes helmet, satisfied)* My mother's useful. She looks after the kid.

MRS. BAILEY   Children are a handicap in times like these. How old is he?

MOLLY   Let me think. I was pregnant the first time two years ago. But I didn't have that one. Then there was a problem in June. Was I pregnant or only late? I'd just as soon have been only late. Then in September. I was sure in November. We got married in January. Duncan went overseas in March. Wait. I've missed out a year. What are we now? August?

JENNY   He's two months old. *(To Willie)* She's got a marvellous memory for everything except that.

WILLIE   You must study, Jenny. You mustn't waste these years. You must learn history, languages.

JENNY   Oh, I do. That's what I spend my money on. The little I earn, that is. I took Russian last winter. An evening course — thirty-seven hours. We learned poetry. Well, one poem.

MOLLY *(At the telephone)* Momma? How's Chuck? What do you mean, all right? I can hear him yelling from here.

JENNY *(To Willie)* It's by a famous poet. Do you want to hear it?

(Reciting)
Alexei! Oh, Alexei!
How bright your eyes did shine
Outside the Lenin Library
Where you said you'd be mine.

Leonid! Oh, Leonid!
I wish I knew you better.
I'm sending you a telegram,
A postcard and a letter.

Vladimir! Oh, Vladimir!
With you I'd love to travel.
I like you more than Fyodor,
Yevgeny, Lev or Pavel.

Nikolai! Oh, Nikolai!

WILLIE Go on.

JENNY That was as far as we got. It was the end of the course. Thirty-seven hours. 'Constructive Russian,' it was called.

MOLLY *(To her mother)* Well, if that's what he seems to want, why don't you give it to him? Or something like it. At that age he won't know the difference. He's only ...

JENNY Two months.

MOLLY Two months old. How much concrete experience do you think he's picked up in two months?

JENNY (*To Willie*) Now that I've finished with Russian I'm studying Strategic Journalism. It's important, it's my whole future. Three classes a week. Then one evening here, taking instruction. That makes four evenings a week. The other three I take Botany, Ethnology, Popular Superstitions, Moths and Butterflies of the British Isles, Bookbinding and Illumination …

WILLIE That seems a heavy educational burden.

JENNY There's nothing else to do at night.

MOLLY (*Covers telephone with her hand and speaks to Willie*) The war, Willie. No men. All gone away. An enormous world with no men in it. None worth looking at twice, that is.

JENNY Don't take that to heart, Willie. You're here. And there's Mr. Gillespie, too.

WILLIE Who's Gillespie?

JENNY The editor of *The Beacon*. His family founded it. It's our finest newspaper. You can see their name, Gillespie, on the masthead. And the family motto, 'O Shed Thy Light'.

MOLLY (*To her mother*) Stop worrying about me. I'm with Jenny Thurstone. We're having ice-cream sodas.

JENNY That's where I work. In the Department of Appraisements and Averages. But it's not where I want to be. I'm trying to get into the Editorial Department.

MOLLY (*To her mother*) You did *not* hear a man's voice. I'm with Jenny.

JENNY   It would be a lot more interesting. And I could do something useful.
(Mrs. Bailey turns on radio)

MRS. BAILEY   Quiet. The news.

RADIO   Legal action has been threatened over last night's blackout which, some people claim, caused, quote, intolerable inconvenience, end quote.

MOLLY   *(To her mother)* I've got to hang up: There's a queue waiting to use the phone. All women.

RADIO   The Anti-Blackout League intends to issue a further statement.

JENNY   *(To Molly)* You leave the tea-cosy off. I have to call Mr. Gillespie.

RADIO   According to the Prime Minister, an annual blackout in wartime is not a sacrifice too great ...

JENNY   *(Dialling)* Lancaster 9875. L-A-N-9-8-7-5. Is that Lancaster 9875?

RADIO   ... Jehovah's Witnesses and other banned organizations were suspected of fomenting the anti-blackout movement ...
(Mrs. Bailey, exasperated, turns radio off)

MRS. BAILEY   *(To Willie)* Are you sure there isn't someone you want to call, too?

WILLIE   I have no friends.

JENNY   Mr. Gillespie? It's Jenny here. Jenny Thurstone, from Appraisements and Averages. Here's news from England — war news. A friend of mine has her husband over there. Lance Corporal ... I *am* getting to the point, Mr. Gillespie.

MRS. BAILEY   *(To Willie)* Do you often have those spells of unconsciousness?

JENNY   Here it is. *(Reading from letter)* The beer in the pubs is too warm and the men are complaining.

MOLLY   Lance-Corporal Duncan Sutherland.

JENNY   Well, I thought it might make a nice little story. I'm sorry, Mr. Gillespie. You've got your son over there ... your boy ... Barry. I'm sorry ... Gary ... Larry ... your boy *Harry*, is it? Never complains. Never a word of ... Proud to do ... Happy to be ... Harry Gillespie. Oh, it *is* Barry. Lieutenant B. Gillespie. You must be proud of him. I can see that. I'm sorry I bothered you. I *really* am. *(Hanging up)* He wasn't interested.

WILLIE   Perhaps it's not a very exciting story.

JENNY   One of the things they tell you in Strategic Journalism is to keep calling editors until they realize your worth.

WILLIE   You're useful where you are. From each according to his ...

JENNY   It's true that I'm good with averages. I once made 99 divided by seven work out to 100. They were pleased.

MOLLY   Can you work out why my husband enlisted?

MRS. BAILEY   *(Ferocious)* To have his own telephone.

MOLLY   He didn't only leave. He left ... me. There's a difference.

WILLIE   To be with his friends.

MOLLY I'm his friend.

JENNY Actually, I do know. I worked it out for an inquiry *The Beacon* ran. 'Why They Enlist.' It turned out to be over food. They weren't getting the ideal meal at home. I worked out the average ideal meal, too. The editors wouldn't accept my conclusion. They wanted me to work it out to 'Hatred of Oppression'. Then they decided 'hatred' sounded negative. They wanted 'Personal Ideals'. Mr. Gillespie turned it down. *(Quoting him)* 'Nobody in his right mind buys a newspaper to read about ideals.' I forget what they finally printed.

MOLLY Can you remember the ideal meal? *(Finds pencil in bag of biscuits. Writes on the back of Duncan's letter)*

MOLLY *(Writing)* Ideal ... meal ... for ... men. Because it *is* men. No woman ever left home over a meal.

JENNY *(Reciting)* Tomato juice or soup.

MOLLY What kind of soup?

JENNY I didn't do the soup breakdown. Olives.

MOLLY *(Writing)* Olives ...

JENNY That's before the soup. I'm sorry. Meat loaf. Flour gravy.

MOLLY *(Giving up)* Some men had that every day of their lives, and they still left.

WILLIE Go on, Jenny. I'd like to hear the whole thing.

JENNY *(Slightly hurt)* Stewed tomatoes.

MRS. BAILEY Anti-Blackout League! Put 'em in jail, where they belong.

JENNY	Buttered carrots. Baked or mashed potatoes.
MRS. BAILEY	Swine. Profiteering swine. The whole lot of 'em.
MOLLY	I've got to leave. My mother gets nervous when I'm late.
JENNY	Hot rolls. Butter.
WILLIE	*(Writing)* Not so fast.
MOLLY	Do you cook, Willie?
JENNY	Chocolate pudding or apple crumble.
MRS. BAILEY	The same crooks who made money out of the Depression are making it now out of the war.
JENNY	Oatmeal cookies.
WILLIE	Chocolate pudding or *what?*
MRS. BAILEY	Their days are numbered.
MOLLY	Jenny. Jenny, come on. It's late.
MRS. BAILEY	Swept aside like dead leaves. And we'll be the brooms.
JENNY	Tea, coffee or milk.
MOLLY	Goodnight, Willie, Goodnight, Mrs. Bailey.
WILLIE	Goodnight, Jenny.
JENNY	Goodnight, Mrs. Bailey. *(Mrs. Bailey turns radio on)*
RADIO	A shortage of sliced pineapple has been reported in some areas. There appears to be no shortage of the crushed. The Prime Minister has issued a statement on the pineapple question: 'If the freedom-loving

peoples of the world want to see sliced pineapple on the dinner-table again, let them buy Victory Bonds.'

Willie, Molly, and Jenny make their goodbyes unheard. Mrs. Bailey, who has started a new helmet, goes on knitting. Willie puts the ideal menu away as if it were a love letter. 'A-Hunting We Will Go' follows news bulletin. Willie covers telephone, starts to hang blanket over window. Stops, looking down to street. Mrs. Bailey lowers music.

MRS. BAILEY   What? *(Jenny and Molly are heard laughing and talking)*

WILLIE   *(To himself)* Goodnight, Jenny.

JENNY   *(From street)* What do you suppose they're talking about?

MRS. BAILEY   Do you happen to remember the fourth rule, Willie?

WILLIE   'No personal feelings.'

MRS. BAILEY   Whoever forgot to make it the first rule ought to be shot.
(Tantivy chorus from 'A-Hunting We Will Go')

SCENE II

Willie's street. Night. Streetlamp. Suggestion of somewhat rundown row houses. Shallow steps. Lamplight. Distant sound of Willie's radio.

JENNY   What do you suppose they're talking about? They've put the blanket over the window again.

MOLLY   *(Lighting cigarette and handing it to Jenny)* Hold that for me, will you? Don't drop it. It's my last one. I've got to go along the street.

JENNY   Molly! You can't.

MOLLY   I can't *here*. There isn't an area.

JENNY   You can't in any area. You don't even know the people.

MOLLY   Would you like me to ring a doorbell and say 'May I pee in your area?'

JENNY   At least pick a different house. Last time I noticed someone twitching a curtain.

MOLLY   Or go back upstairs and ask Willie?

JENNY   No, you can't. I'd die of shame. *(As Molly goes off)* Molly, not there. Not there. They'll remember you from last time. Molly! They're twitching the curtain again.

MOLLY   *(Off)* We forgot to ask Willie about the difference between Leninist expansion and pan-Slavism.

JENNY Oh, come back, come back. Somebody might think it's me. *(Drops Molly's cigarette and steps on it)*

MOLLY *(Saunters back, straightening her clothing)* Think it's you doing what?

JENNY Smoking in the street.

Molly sits on Willie's steps. Spills everything out of the paper bag. Finds a pack of cigarettes. Puts everything back except cigarette, and a large, tatty, yellowed pamphlet in Russian.

MOLLY Lucky for you I had another pack. I'd have throttled you.

JENNY Oh, you've brought it. You've brought it!

Jenny sinks down beside Molly and reverently takes the pamphlet.

MOLLY It was all my father had to leave me. My entire inheritance.

JENNY But what an inheritance. Where did he get it? *(Turns pages as though examining pictures rather than print)*

MOLLY He won it off a Ukrainian merchant seaman in a poker game.

JENNY Your father could read Russian, of course. *(Molly doubts this)*

JENNY *(As if reading title)*
What ... Is... To ... Be ... Done?' That must be what it says.

MOLLY Unless it's 'by V. I. Lenin.'

JENNY It would depend on their publishing tradition. Whether they put the title first. It could be 'What Is

	To Be Done?' by V.I. Lenin or V.I. Lenin's 'What Is To Be Done?'
MOLLY	You should know. You had thirty-seven hours of Constructive Russian.
JENNY	That was a different vocabulary. *(Returning pamphlet)* It's been worth living eighteen years just to hold this. I've brought something to show you, too. *(Gives Molly a photograph)*
MOLLY	*(Holds it to light or streetlamp)* What is it?
JENNY	My father.
MOLLY	Was he always in skirts?
JENNY	He's barely three years old there.
MOLLY	Are you sure it's not your mother? The dress. And the long curls.
JENNY	That was my father, G. E. Thurstone. When I knew him his hair was short. Quite short, in fact.
MOLLY	What's G. and E.?
JENNY	George and Edward. Of course.
MOLLY	They've tied the poor little bugger to a locomotive. Like a living sacrifice.
JENNY	It was a train just about to make its first run on a line in Northern India.
MOLLY	He's sitting on the Union Jack.
JENNY	The locomotive was decorated. It was a festive first run.
MOLLY	You mean they tied that poor little boy — if it was a boy — to a Union Jack and tied the Union Jack to

	a locomotive and sent the whole thing hurtling off into the wilds of Asia?
JENNY	He liked remembering it. It wasn't a fast train.
MOLLY	What a monstrous thing to do to a kid.
JENNY	He didn't think so.
MOLLY	I'm trying to imagine my own father. Mick McCormack at the age of three tied to a locomotive about to make its first run from Cork to Bantry. Sitting on a flag. No. I can't see it.
JENNY	Your father was different. A fighter. A real revolutionary. *(With profound admiration)* A real deserter. From the Navy.
MOLLY	*(Reciting easily)* Deserted in 1916. Came out here wearing just the clothes he was standing up in.

Mick McCormack, aged about 22, emerges. This is not a ghost story and he is not a ghost; he is a figure described by Molly and imagined by Jenny. Mick wears a Russian sailor uniform. Mutiny on the Potemkin.

JENNY	A rebel. A fighter.
MOLLY	Oh, he was that, all right. It was a fight that finally killed him.
JENNY	Fighting for justice. *The Storming of the Winter Palace.*
MOLLY	*(As if trying to recall something said on another occasion)* Officially, an industrial accident.
JENNY	*(Reciting a fairy story got by heart)* Your mother was left destitute. You were evicted.
MOLLY	That's true enough, God knows. *Mick fades.*

JENNY   You moved into a damp, miserable room filled with bedbugs.

MOLLY   Ah, the bugs. I can still see them. Armies marching in formation across the ceiling. All they needed was fife and drum.

JENNY   You and your mother went hungry. You had anemia. TB. Rickets.

MOLLY   Chronic hiccoughs. I had chronic hiccoughs, too. *(Unconsciously reproducing a childhood accent)* Me mother's teeth fell out. She did look a hag.

JENNY   You were lucky. You got off to a good start.

MOLLY   *(Looking at photograph)* What about Curlytop? Why'd he leave England?

JENNY   He wasn't awfully good about passing exams. So he came here. They made him a school inspector.

MOLLY   Oh. Jesus, don't I remember the kind!

G. E. Thurstone, remittance man, as Molly would see him. Seedy, boozy, obtuse, but rather splendid. Defiantly English clothes, that is, to a North American eye in 1942, casual, sloppy, unpressed.

G. E. THURSTONE   Spell 'ate'.

CHILD'S VOICE   *(Spelling what it hears)* E-T.

G. E. THURSTONE   Wrong. Spell 'Nelson'.

CHILD'S VOICE   N-L-S-N. Nlsn.

G. E. THURSTONE   Wrong. Spell 'hounds'.

CHILD'S VOICE   H-A-N-D-S.

G. E. THURSTONE   Wrong. Think! 'The hounds are in their kennels'.

CHILD'S VOICE   The hands are in their knls.

G. E. THURSTONE   Spell arse.
    (Silence) Wrong, wrong, and wrong again.

JENNY   He seemed to feel he was in the Congo and couldn't understand the tribal tongues. But nobody understood his.

MOLLY   Did he have any friends?

JENNY   He had me. But I think he was lonely.

MOLLY   I suppose he kept looking for his own kind.

G. E. THURSTONE   *(As to dog)* Down, sir!

JENNY   He gave me what he could. Within his limits. He gave me books ... and music ... and drawing ... and dancing ... and French ... and riding ... and ...

MOLLY   You've had a lot to overcome.

JENNY   He forgot to tell me there was no money. *(On which G. E. Thurstone disappears)* And he died. Oh, not like your father. Not fighting. No, he just gradually vanished. Like an old photograph that's been left in a harsh light.

MOLLY   You've still got a mother. I've always lived with mine.

JENNY   Well, you see, mine married someone. A Mr. Herbert.

MOLLY   You sound as though you hardly knew him.

JENNY   He plays golf in warm climates. He and my mother come here sometimes. They've invited me ... but ... she doesn't understand about my working. She doesn't understand the difference between working for a lark and for a living.

MOLLY I'm holding Duncan's job for him. There's nothing to it. He'll never again be able to come home at night saying he's tired. I'll say to him, I'll say, 'Listen, Jack ...'

JENNY Duncan. His name is Duncan.

MOLLY 'Jack' is for emphasis.

JENNY I read Duncan's letter. The last paragraph.

MOLLY I thought you might. Keep your mind off that subject.

JENNY It's not what you think. Not at all. I only want to know because ... because I don't know.

MOLLY Once you know you'll wish you didn't. You'll long for the great days when you were only wondering.

JENNY Why do you stay married, then?

MOLLY *(Glancing up at Willie's window)*
His window's open. He's taken the blanket away.
(Begins throwing everything back in the paper bag)
Mrs. Bailey must be on her way down. You can keep the pamphlet until next week, if you like.

JENNY And you can keep my father's picture. Just for the week.

MOLLY I wish we had a place where we could talk. Really talk, without being interrupted all the time.

JENNY I wish I didn't live in a room. I'm not allowed visitors. Not even girls. Not even children.

MOLLY I've got my mother at home. She never goes out, except to Mass.

JENNY   Did you mean it?

MOLLY   About my mother?

JENNY   About wishing we could talk.

MOLLY   What's wrong with that?

JENNY   I believe what people tell me. I believe you. I believe Willie.

MOLLY   *(Imitating Willie)*
'It is a wise rule to have no friends at all.' He's probably found friendship too dangerous. He's mixed it up with love. He's afraid of promissory notes. But nothing is owed in friendship. You can close the account without publishing a statement. No one can claim a right to examine the books. There are no mortgages.

JENNY   And love?

MOLLY   Just one foreclosure after another.

JENNY   *(Warning)* Mrs. Bailey!

Jenny and Molly hide in the dark, leaving the paper bag. Mrs. Bailey, who has nearly finished the new helmet, continues to knit as she walks. The Carmen-Escamilla duo bursts out of Willie's window. Mrs. Bailey looks up. Disapproves.

MRS. BAILEY   I don't mind noise. I don't even mind music. It's the meaning ... the meaning. Love. Love. No objection to love. Only, love isn't progress. It's in the natural order, but not in the natural movement. The natural movement goes ... well ... from religion to politics. That's a natural movement. Where's love? Before religion, if you like. To one side. A kind of

by-pass. Somewhere. But not between. Not between religion and politics. For one thing, there's no room. *(Accidentally knocks over the bag of biscuits)*
Try to tell *them* that. They'll never be useful. It's all been handed to them on a platter. There's no progression. No natural ... *(Pause) Our* progress ... you can trace it. One landmark after another. First, 'Jesus Loves Me.' Subjective. Then, 'I'm On the Rock to Stay, Hallelujah.' Affirmative. Then in no time it was, 'Oh, You Can't Scare Me. I'm Sticking with the Union.' Perceptive. After that it was 'Red Flag' before you could wink, and 'The Internationale' in tune, good timing, breath controlled, the rhythm mastered. Ping, ping, ping ... *(Hums the first six notes)* Catch one of them doing that. Heart's in the right place. But a tin ear. Tin ear for the future.

(Brief discouragement)
Will never be useful. Can't think of one who will ever be useful. Try to hold things together. Keep trying. Keep trying. *(Still faithfully knitting, shuffles off)*

SCENE III

New Year's Eve at the Austro-Hungarian Friendship Club.
Jenny, Molly, Barman.

A shabby bar. A radio, a wind-up phonograph, a few records, a telephone. On the wall a large picture of Kaiser Franz Josef II.

Signs:
AUSTRO-HUNGARIAN FRIENDSHIP CLUB.
MEMBERS ONLY!
REMEMBER MAYERLING.
VICTORY IN 1943.

Barman in shirtsleeves. Wears a revolver in a holster. Jenny and Molly alone at a table. Three empty white wine bottles on the floor beside them. A fresh bottle on the table. Slight change in hairstyles: they have been making an effort with curlers and pins. Unsophisticated. Dresses bright in colour, with matching jackets or boleros they have now taken off. They wear snow-boots. Coats, hats and scarves on a coat rack, along with a number of winter coats evidently belonging to men.

Last strains of the overture to 'Die Fledermaus.' Barman winds up phonograph and starts overture again from the beginning.

MOLLY   Put your jacket on. You look naked. They're coming over again.

JENNY   How many?

MOLLY   Only one. Cover up. Don't look. Keep your head down.

Molly stretches out a leg, indicates her snow boot, as if explaining why she can't dance.

JENNY   Has he gone?

MOLLY   I think he just wanted to dance.

JENNY   With both of us?

MOLLY   You can look now. No, don't. Don't look. They're fighting. At the other end of the room. *(Pushes Jenny's head down. A crash)*

JENNY   What was it?

MOLLY   Only a table. It missed us by at least a foot. *(Confused sound of shouts, broken glass, smashed furniture. Barman fires gun in the air)*
(No effect, hastily changes record. First bars of 'Radetzky March.' Instant silence)

MOLLY   We'd better stand up. They're all at attention.

JENNY   The Radetzky March. I wonder who Radetzky was?

MOLLY   Radetzky was a bastard. Stop smiling. You'll have them swarming over here again. We're the only women in the place.

JENNY   I'm trying to show political solidarity without being sexually provocative.

MOLLY   You're not succeeding.

BARMAN   *(At their table)*
Who did you two girls say you were waiting for?

JENNY We didn't say we were waiting for anyone. We're friends of Mr. Willie Howe. He used to come here with his German friend, Karl-Heinz something. But Karl-Heinz has been interned, now. Because of the war.

BARMAN I've already told you, we aren't allowed to serve unaccompanied women.

MOLLY We are accompanied. We're with each other.

BARMAN If your boyfriends don't show up, you'll have to leave.

MOLLY Why? Are we drunk? Are we throwing tables?

JENNY We just came in to talk.

BARMAN The Austro-Hungarian Friendship Club on New Year's Eve is no place for conversation.

MOLLY *(Slips him a tip)* Make us temporary members. Pretend we're men.

BARMAN Do me a favour. Keep away from the men. The real men. I don't want the police in here.

MOLLY *(To Jenny)* Are you sure this is the right place?

JENNY It's working-class and it's European. Of course it's left wing! What else could it be?

MOLLY There must be gaps in Willie's instruction.

BARMAN Quiet! The news.

JENNY You see? Just like Mrs. Bailey.
(Dead silence)

RADIO *(Squeaks and waits of shortwave. Voice speaking in the precise English of foreign announcers)*

VOICE ... in the words of the leader, 1943 will be the year of final, total, and unconditional victory for

Western civilization. Enemy forces are cringing and retreating on all fronts ... from the Atlantic to the Urals ... and beyond ... 1943 ... Victory ...
(Voice fades. Lively shortwave chorus of 'Bomben auf Engeland' mingled with cheering in the bar)

MOLLY   I think we'd better leave.

JENNY   I thought you wanted a place where we could talk.

MOLLY   Where we could *what?*

JENNY   TALK.
(Voices in bar singing 'Erika', with stamping of feet. Jenny talks to Molly unheard. Singing fades. Jenny heard plainly)

JENNY   I called Mr. Gillespie. I told him about Willie's friend. Mr. Gillespie, I said here is a man who fought in Spain ... who fought against Hitler ... and what have we done with him, I said. Locked him up in a camp.
(Engulfed by chorus of 'Erika')

JENNY   Mr. Gillespie said, he said it can't be true. Mr. Gillespie, I said, there's bus service practically up to the barbed wire. If it is true, Mr. Gillespie said, if it is true, if we have got camps in this country, it must be because of the damned war.
('Erika')

JENNY   Wars always bring on lower-class immigration, Mr. Gillespie said. The scum of Central Europe has been dumped over here. Besides, he said, if we do have camps, you can bet your boots they're decent. Are you trying to compare us to the Germans, he said.
(Last bars of 'Erika')

JENNY   So I just wished him a Happy New Year.

MOLLY   You didn't mention Willie, I hope.

JENNY   Not to Mr. Gillespie. Only to the police.
(Seems surprised at Molly's reaction)
Willie told me about this club, this place where German refugees meet. I didn't ask Willie for the address. He might have wanted to come too, and it would just be like instruction. Instead of talk. So I've got the makings of a reporter, Molly. I really have. I thought, if anyone knows where a private drinking club is, it's the police. So I rang them up.

MOLLY   Did you give your name?

JENNY   Not in so many words. Anyway, here we are. We can talk without being interrupted. Nobody knows we're here.

Barman puts on the 'Auf der Jagd' polka. Jenny and Molly argue intensely, unheard. They are gradually distracted by the music. Then drawn. Take off their jackets. Their boots. Finally jump up impulsively and dance. Wild, cheerful, funny, coarse. Barman shoots his gun and then applauds.

JENNY   Oh, Molly, Molly! Nothing can stop me! Nothing can get in my way! If my head were cut off I'd grow a new one.

MOLLY   My head was lopped when Duncan left. It's too late for me to grow anything new.

JENNY   You might meet someone else. That would be new.

MOLLY   I was born faithful.

JENNY   Is that good?

MOLLY   In times like these, it's a handicap.

JENNY   What about Duncan? Is he ... you know ... faithful?

MOLLY   The girls over there. They lurk in doorways, in the blackout. They drag men in off the street.

JENNY   Duncan would put up a fight.

MOLLY   He keeps repeating, 'No, no, I love my wife.'

JENNY   In doorways. Molly?

MOLLY   Standing up.

JENNY   Standing up?

MOLLY   It must be like being raped in an Egyptian tomb.

JENNY   That could never happen unless you wanted it.

MOLLY   I wanted curly hair but it came out straight. I never wanted Duncan to leave. I didn't want a kid, but my mother's a grandmother.

JENNY   How long does it take? What you just said.

MOLLY   Unless you have elephants in mind, nine months.

JENNY   Not that. I know that. I mean, how long does *it* take. *It.*

MOLLY   *(Once she realizes Jenny means this)*
Having been born faithful, I'll never know if it can take more than ten minutes.

JENNY   There's never been anything published? No statistic?

MOLLY   Why don't you take the whole thing over and work out the average?

JENNY   Would that be useful?

MOLLY   Ask Mrs. Bailey.

JENNY   It's not a thing Willie ever mentioned.

MOLLY   I should hope not. If he ever does, if he ever so much as hints ...

JENNY   When you were my age, you'd been pregnant twice and late thirteen times.

MOLLY   Exactly.

BARMAN   *(Answering telephone)* One of you girls called 'Molly'?

MOLLY   Mother? How's Charlie? Well, if he doesn't want that one, give him one like it. How should I know where to find one? Ask the neighbours. That was not a man who answered. It was *not* a man. It was Jenny's father, Mr. Thurstone. We helped him inspect a school, then we all went to Vespers. Well, it's up to you to prove I'm lying. You're the one making the accusation.

JENNY   I thought nobody knew where we were.

Mrs. Bailey comes in, seen by Molly but not by Jenny.

MOLLY   My mother has to know. I've got a kid.

JENNY   Will he always need to know where you are? Will Duncan?

MOLLY   Always. Though they may know by instinct. Like Mrs. Bailey.

Mrs. Bailey takes off her coat, hangs it up. Advances confidently. Sits down with Jenny and Molly.

BARMAN   *(To Mrs. Bailey)* You over twenty-one?

Mrs. Bailey knits without replying. Barman points to sign.

BARMAN Members only. This is a private drinking club. Registered with the police.

Jenny looks at Molly as if to say, 'There , I told you so'.

BARMAN You gotta be a member.

MRS. BAILEY Young man, I am a member.

BARMAN Show me your card.

MRS. BAILEY My what?

BARMAN Show me your membership card.

MRS. BAILEY That's disgusting.

JENNY It's a Fascist demand.

MOLLY *(To Jenny)* Shut up, for God's sake.

BARMAN *(Softly)* I just need to see your card.

MRS. BAILEY Keep your voice down.

BARMAN I'm not supposed to serve unaccompanied women. Two was bad enough. Now there's three of you.

MOLLY *(To Jenny. Extremely troubled)* Tell me exactly what you said to the police. Whose name did you mention? What did you say?

JENNY I said I was a star reporter on *The Beacon*.

BARMAN Are there still more of you? More women?

MRS. BAILEY You'll see when the time comes.

MOLLY A fight! A fight! They're fighting! *(Barman hastily puts on 'The Radetzky March', almost immediately looks at his watch. Stops record)*

BARMAN It is now ... 1943!
(All embrace. Applause and cheers)

BARMAN *(Climbs on bar. Lifting glass)*
   To our total and unconditional victory in 1943!
   (Cheers)
   From the Atlantic to the Urals!

JENNY   And beyond!

BARMAN To the annihilation of the barbarian hordes! To the triumph of Western culture!

JENNY   *(Standing on table)*
   To civilization!

BARMAN The new order!

JENNY   The new life!

BARMAN One Europe!
   (Cheers)

JENNY   One world!

BARMAN The world our friends are dying for!

JENNY   The only world worth living for!

BARMAN Our world!

JENNY   One world. Our world. The world of ... SOCIALIST MARXIST REVOLUTION. *(Barman puts on 'The Radetzky March.' Gestures to the three to get out)*

MRS. BAILEY   Now you've done it.

MOLLY   Come on. While they're at attention.

JENNY   Now I've done what?

MOLLY   I told you Radetzky was a bastard.

Molly and Mrs. Bailey push and pull Jenny out, grabbing coats, hats, snowboots, as they go. Barman keeps gun trained on customers. Molly dashes back, snatches bottle off the table.

MOLLY   What's more, we resign our temporary membership!

Molly runs off. Barman stops 'The Radetzky March', puts on overture to 'Die Fledermaus'. Puts gun back in holster. Turns picture of Kaiser Franz Josef II around, revealing portrait of Adolf Hitler. Pours champagne, swaying in time to the music, as cheers and happy voices rise and mingle with the waltz.

SCENE IV

Summer 1943. Jenny's new apartment.

Sunday. Church bells.

Plain white room. Window with lopsided Venetian blind. Sunlight. Paintpots with brushes, black and white. Painted on wall: SECOND FRO — unfinished, like everything in the room. No furniture — that is, no bed, table or chairs. Whatever she owns is on the floor: books, a mattress, a few cushions, some of her clothes, wire coat-hangers, a telephone, a directory. A radio and a toaster, both on the floor, are plugged into the same power-point. Upon a wooden packing case, a teapot, a coffeepot, a milk bottle, ready-sliced bread in a bright wrapper.

Jenny's hair is tied back with a ribbon. Her dress is somehow more careless than last summer's. Her feet are bare.

She is engaged in a hopeless attempt at tidying the room. She does not walk — she dances. This is not affectation but pure happiness.

Church bells die away. Sound of child bouncing a ball in the street just outside the window.

CHILD	St. James, St... John and good St. Mark sailed off with Noah in the Ark. They took a ton of wine to drink, and Rita Hayworth wearing mink.
JENNY	*(While she speaks, one can see the child's ball occasionally tossed in the air outside the window)* This place is mine. The whole thing. The walls.

The floor, the window, the doorbell. I have a telephone number — Wilbank 1514. I answer every time it rings. You can call me whenever you want to, even at night. I answer all the wrong numbers, because it's my phone. The Venetian blind is mine. I paid for it. You can have it halfway up or halfway down, but never right up or right down. It doesn't — well, you can see that it doesn't. The four wire coat-hangers are mine. *(Holds them up)* I bought them. The teapot, the mattress, the pillows — mine. I haven't any sheets or blankets yet, but the weather's been quite hot. The whole thing, lease included, for two hundred dollars.

You're probably wondering where I got the money. It was Mr. Gillespie's idea — the Heartfelt Empire Poem Contest. Five hundred dollar first prize. Staff members weren't eligible, so I used Mrs. Bailey's name. That was *her* idea. From each according to his abilities. I won. I mean, we won. She won. Her half-share came to three hundred dollars. She gave me two. That was how I came to own the coat-hangers.

I'm not too happy about the contest, artistically speaking. It's not up to me to ... I'll just give you the lines I did *not* write.

'Oh dearest island, wrapped in mist,
I've got you first upon my list.'
I never wrote that. And I did not write,
'I cherish every palm and pine;
Consider me your Valentine', either. Those lines were not the work of Jenny Thurstone. That's all I wish to say about the Heartfelt Empire poem

episode.
(Doorbell. Jenny answers)

VOICE   Have you found Jesus?

JENNY   I can't invite you in this time — there's no place to sit. But another time I'd be glad to. *(Returns carrying a pile of pamphlets)* I'm on the ground floor, you see, and they often think I'm the caretaker.

Child's ball bounces in the window. Jenny picks it up and goes to window. Tosses it to the child. Looking up, she glances across the street.

Oh! Stop it. Stop it. It's terrible. Stop! Wait. Don't be frightened. I'm coming to help you.

Rushes to door, changes her mind, kneels beside the telephone, looking frantically through the directory.

E ... F ... G ... G ... Gabor ... Gabriel ... Galaxy Termite Disposal Limited ... General Motors ... Gibson ... Gilbert ... Gillespie. Gillespie. Albert ... Bertrans, Curtains and Draperies ... Gillespie Druids and Warlocks. It can't be ... he would have mentioned it. Dwight. That's it. Dwight Gillespie. Oh, it's terrible. Terrible. Mr. Gillespie? It's Jenny. Jenny, from Appraisements and Averages. Yes ... well, actually, I do know it's Sunday. That's why I thought you'd be at home. Don't hang up — I just want to tell you this one thing. They're stoning some Jehovah's Witnesses in my street. Here, here, I can see it... Just across from ... well, I just think someone should write about it. Someone should ... They're not what? They're not Christians? *(Reaches over and picks up a pamphlet)* Well, they say they are. Real Christians keep out of trouble? Yes. Well. I suppose you must be right. It's just — they're across the street, in a doorway. You can hear the people yelling. *(Holds telephone up to window)* I've never seen it before. I've never seen people with their arms over their faces ... and other people throwing stones. I want to ... to help. Then I thought ... Mr. Gillespie, you're quite wrong about me. I *am* a Christian. Real Christians mind their own god-damned business? I expect you're right. I mean, you'd know. You must be forty. Forty-five even. Forty-seven? My God. I'm sorry, Mr. Gillespie. *(Police siren heard)* It's all right. It seems to be over. I'm sorry. *(Hangs up. Looks out)* They've arrested the Jehovah's Witnesses. *(Examines pamphlet)* Apparently this is all subversive stuff about the Heavenly Kingdom. *(Lets the pamphlet fall and forgets it instantly)* The radio's mine. And the toaster. The radio's useful in case you want to hear the news in English.

(Turns on radio, which emits whistles and static, then tantivy chorus of 'A-Hunting We Will Go')

RADIO   *(Ever cheerful)*
A turning point in North Africa was ... turned ... today when the oasis of Muzzluk fell to Allied forces, after a siege lasting seven months. The entire population of the oasis ... at least, what's left of it ...

JENNY   That's how you get news in English. Over the radio. If you want news in French, you have to put bread in the toaster.

(Puts bread in toaster. Sound of alarm bell, then Yvonne Printemps singing 'Je t'aime, Je t'aime!')

TOASTER   This morning, Maréchal Pétain attended Mass in Vichy, France. A large crowd stood waiting outside the church to cheer him. The Maréchal blessed the crowd and performed several miracles. Generalissimo Francisco Franco attended Mass in Madrid. No miracles were reported. Signor Benito Mussolini attended services in Rome, Florence, Milan, Venice, Genoa, Turin and Naples. The Duce left instructions for miracles to be worked in his absence. That was the war news. *('Je t'aime, Je t'aime!')*

JENNY   But there's one thing you must never do and that is try to have English news and toast at the same time. If you do, all the lights blow out. *(Demonstrates. Removes toast, butters it, eats it. Begins painting the letter N after FRO)*

RADIO   Enemy troops are said to have reached the Earls. The Yearls. The Yurruls. The U-R-A-L-S. A range of mountains. *(Red Army musical medley)*

SCENE V

January 1944. Second Front Rally.

Red Army medley, stirring and clear. This fades, and voices are heard singing to a piano. The doleful keening of the righteous.

> Song   We're marching with Stalin.
> *(Piano thumps)*
> We're marching with Churchill.
> *(Piano)*
> We're marching with Chiang Kai-Shek ...

Assembly hall. Could be a slightly rundown Protestant school borrowed for a patriotic evening. On the wall clusters of flags, Red Flag, Union Jack, loops of bunting in the particularly hideous red manufactured for such occasions. Three portraits: Stalin; the Royal Family (George VI, Queen Elizabeth, and the two Princesses); and an unknown man in a bowler hat. Slogans: SECOND FRONT RALLY and GOD BLESS THE RED ARMY! A pay phone. Winter overcoats piled on a chair. On top of the pile, a number of Mrs. Bailey's knitted helmets, in bright, distinctive colours. Sitting side by side on plain chairs, Mrs. Bailey, Willie, Jenny and Molly, singing from mimeographed song sheets. Marked change in Willie's dress. Much sharper suit and a bright tie.

> Mrs. Bailey   That's not marching. You're dragging your feet.

JENNY   It's just that Chiang Kai-Shek doesn't fit the tune. Can't we sing 'de Gaulle'? De Gaulle would fit.

MOLLY   And it's pitched too high for Willie.
(Piano thumps)

JENNY   They're starting again.

ALL FOUR   We're marching with Staaalin ...

JENNY   Some people are singing 'with Roosevelt'.

Mrs. Bailey looks around. Notices a slogan on the wall. Eases out of the row, takes down GOD.

MOLLY   Nobody understood the Archbishop. Nobody understands one word. It was like an English movie. For the first five minutes you might as well be deaf.

JENNY   I understood.

MOLLY   What did he say?

JENNY   That we were all friends.

MOLLY   No one applauded.

JENNY   I did.

MRS. BAILEY   Sing, sing. The crowd's getting restless.
(Sings) With Chuuuuurchill ...

JENNY   Why are they late? We've been singing the same thing for twenty minutes. The Archbishop was on time.

WILLIE   *(Glasgow much less pronounced)* They've come all the way from Stalingrad.

MOLLY   The Archbishop came all the way from Canterbury. He was on time.

JENNY Maybe they couldn't find a taxi once they got here. Oh. God. Oh God. Here they are. Oh Molly. They're here. We're looking at two Red Army colonels. Two of them. From Stalingrad. Molly! Molly!

(Prolonged applause, then all four sit down to hear the Colonels speak)

JENNY It was worth living to be here at this moment. *(Silence)*

MOLLY What's he saying?

MRS. BAILEY Hush.

MOLLY Come on, Jenny. You took Constructive Russian. What's he saying?

JENNY That was a different vocabulary. *(Silence)*

JENNY They're a bit ... a bit on the stout side. *(Frown from Mrs. Bailey)* And they grin such a lot. Colonels shouldn't grin.

WILLIE *(Quietly)* Or wear civilian shoes.

MOLLY D'you see the gold teeth, Jenny? The little fellow. Solid gold.

JENNY So fat. So old.

MOLLY He's got a million dollars worth of gold right there in his mouth.

MRS. BAILEY Stand up. On your feet! A standing ovation! *(All stand. Willie does not applaud)*

JENNY They're taking their caps off. That's a nice gesture.

MOLLY They should have kept them on. Bald heroes.

MRS. BAILEY   I've never heard a crowd like this ... Stamping! Screaming!

JENNY   *(Clapping)* They're coming back.

MOLLY   If you don't know what they said, why are you clapping?

JENNY   They brought us a message. I understood that.

WILLIE   What was the message, Jenny?

JENNY   Truth, justice, courage, love. Never give up. Never give in. I don't care about their shoes. I don't care if they're fat, old, bald, anything.

MOLLY   But the *teeth*.

JENNY   I don't care. I don't care. *(Waving)* Goodbye! Goodbye!

MRS. BAILEY   Jenny's heart's in the right place.

JENNY   *(With deep confidence)* And I'm useful.
(All relax. Rally over)

WILLIE   A couple of apparatchiks. From the Soviet Embassy.

MRS. BAILEY   *(Warning)* They were flown here from Stalingrad, at great danger to themselves and great expense to us.

Willie begins to gather up the music sheets and take down the flags. Takes down the word RED, leaving BLESS THE ARMY.

MRS. BAILEY   *(Noticing this)* Just leave it, Willie.

WILLIE   I'm on the cleanup committee.

JENNY   It's all right. We'll finish, you do look tired, Willie.

Jenny takes no further notice of Willie. Not cruel, but innocent. Willie slowly disentangles his coat from the pile on the chair. Waits. Nothing. No one notices when he leaves.

MRS. BAILEY   *(To Jenny and Molly)* You may keep the decorations. As souvenirs. *(Generously)* And ... and a couple of helmets.

JENNY   Thank you, Mrs. Bailey.

Mrs. Bailey puts on coat and hat. Takes down picture of unknown man wearing bowler hat and goes off.

MOLLY   Funny she didn't take Stalin.

JENNY   It was kind of her to leave him for us. Who was the other man? Some great leader?

MOLLY   That was her father, Burned-out Benson. He was a famous arsonist. Died in jail, in a fire he set himself. She hangs his picture whenever she gets the chance. In Memoriam.

JENNY   She's very loyal.

MOLLY   Do you want Stalin or the Royal Family?

JENNY   Just as you like.

MOLLY   We can toss. Got a coin? *(Jenny gives her a coin. Molly tosses, catches, slaps the coin on the back of her hand three times)* Heads. Tails. Heads. Two out of three. I win.

JENNY   You never said. You never said ...

MOLLY   You weren't listening. *(Molly pockets the coin. Jenny takes down the pictures. Gives Stalin to Molly)*

MOLLY   Let's trade.

JENNY   *(Surprised)* All right.

MOLLY *(Considering BLESS THE ARMY)* I don't think much of that. Which army? It could be the wrong one. *(Removes ARMY)* That's even worse.

JENNY It all has to come down anyway.

MOLLY It should have real meaning until the end. *(Removes THE)* Bless. Bless. It stands on its own. I'll keep GOD as a souvenir.

JENNY I'll take a word, too.

MOLLY What does that give us? I've got God and the Royal Family.

JENNY I've got Stalin and 'The'.

MOLLY One of us is overprivileged. *(Taking down bunting)* What's God to you?

JENNY George the Fifth. Of course.

MOLLY Mine's a farmer. A cunning old peasant who owns all the land in Right. We meet at fairs and make deals. I promise him this, he lets me have that. He usually wins.

JENNY Have you gone back to the Church, Molly?

MOLLY It's got nothing to do with religion. This is just horse trading between two smart operators, one of whom happens to be invisible. I've just made my most important bargain. If Duncan survives, if he isn't killed. I've promised to change.

JENNY Into what?

MOLLY Into whatever he imagined he married … I've thought and thought and I don't see how else it can work.

Jenny	But you're perfect, Molly. A perfect friend. A perfect comrade.
Molly	'Wife' is something else.
Jenny	I could work it out for you — average perfect wife.
Molly	I don't need it worked out. I'm not a statistic. I'm married to Duncan. I've got to live with him for something like fifty years.
Jenny	Fifty years. *(This is beyond her — why anyone would want such a thing?)* Molly, who were those two, really? The two Colonels.
Molly	You heard Willie.
Jenny	What about the Archbishop?
Molly	I didn't get a look at his shoes.
Jenny	It doesn't matter. I don't care. What matters is what I felt when I believed. When I thought it was true. I've never been so happy.
Molly	That's marriage. Now you know.
Jenny	You promised ... remember? That we'd be together. The three of us. You and Duncan and me. To build the new world. The only world worth living for ... you said.
Molly	Yes. Is there a phone here?
Jenny	A pay phone.
Molly	Got a coin?
Jenny	*(Wants to say something, but thinks it unworthy)* I think so.
Molly	*(To her mother. Exceptionally raffinée)* Is that you, Mummy? Good. And Charles. Charles. Your grandson. That's tiresome of him. If it seems to be

what he wants, you might as well let him have it. But not all at once. I'm with Jenny. We've been to see 'How to Build an Igloo'.

Molly starts to put her coat on. Jenny, now dressed in boots, hat and coat sits contemplating Stalin…

MOLLY   What is it, Jenny? Would you rather have the Royal Family?

JENNY   What if I never have anything else?

MOLLY   You mean than Stalin?

JENNY   In a way.

MOLLY   You could have Willie, too, if you wanted him.

JENNY   Willie's nice. Did you fall in love with Duncan because he was nice?

MOLLY   Oh, Jenny. *(Sits down, leaving a chair empty between them)* None of us ever fell in love with a man because he was nice.

JENNY   I was wondering.

MOLLY   Duncan knows about you. He knows our plans include you.

JENNY   I'm not looking for a family. I'm looking for a life.

MOLLY   There's no We anywhere. There's a war.

JENNY   But after. First thing.

MOLLY   Then we get rid of Stalin.

JENNY   Molly!

MOLLY   Franco, I meant.

JENNY   *(Happy)* Then we can go away. The three of us.

MOLLY   Yes.

JENNY   To make the world you promised.

MOLLY   The world my father promised. Or was it *your* father, G. E. Thurstone? *(Break in tension. The verge of uncontrollable laughter)*

JENNY   Mrs. Bailey's father.

MOLLY   The world of Burned-out Benson.

JENNY   Get rid of Benson.

MOLLY   Get rid of Mrs. Bailey.

JENNY   What you said. It was so funny. 'Get rid of Stalin.'

MOLLY   Get rid of Churchill.

JENNY   It was so funny. I never in my whole life heard anything so funny. 'Get rid of Stalin.'

MOLLY   Make Stalin governor-general of Bermuda.

JENNY   It doesn't fit ... it doesn't fit the music.

MOLLY   Stalin is pitched too high for Willie.

JENNY   Stop it ... I'll die. Get ... Get rid ... Get rid of ...

Abruptly stop laughing. Seem bewildered. Refugees sitting in the wrong railway station. Two orphans waiting to be claimed. First one, then the other, hums 'The Internationale'. Jenny knows a few words, Molly a few more. Sad. Wistful. Nostalgic. Could be 'La Vie en Rose'; 'Rock of Ages'; 'Love's Old Sweet Song'.

SCENE VI

June 1944. Jenny, Molly.

Jenny's apartment. A few improvements: a day-bed, a couple of chairs. The slogan on the wall now reads SECOND FRON. In evidence: One of Willie's Spanish War posters, and the picture of Burned-out Benson in his bowler hat. A packing crate still does as a table. A few flowers in a milk bottle. A collection of other bottles — gin, Scotch and so on — on the windowsill. Paintpots have not been moved. Radio, telephone and toaster still live on the floor.

Molly is 22, Jenny 20. Dresses tightly belted. Summer sandals with high heels. Hair swept up in front and long behind. Greater change in Molly than Jenny. White handbag. Red fingernails. Makeup.

Jenny is making a stab at clearing rubbish off the crate so that she can set out teacups.

Molly stands, holding the telephone. Chic new way of standing. When she says a few words in French, her voice rises an octave.

> MOLLY   Allo, allo, allo! C'est toi, ma petite Maman? C'est moi. Moi. Molly. MOLLY. Et le petit Charles? Tell him his petite Maman ... no, *his* petite Maman ... well, I don't mean the mother of Charles de Gaulle. He wants what? It seems to me that if he has indicated his choice clearly ... understands every possible consequence of his decision ... I'm with

Jenny. No, there are no men here. Listen. *(Holds telephone at arm's length)* There, did you hear a man? Au revoir, ma petite Maman cherie!

Jenny removes miscellany of objects from a chair so that Molly can sit down.

JENNY   Mrs. Bailey gave me her father's picture. Now that she's being analyzed she says she doesn't need him. She took Stalin instead. Willie gave me the tea-cosy. He never uses it now. The poster ... he's moved to a new place where you aren't allowed to hang posters. You're only allowed very good reproductions ... like ... Picasso, but just the Blue Period. I think I've done something wrong about tea.

MOLLY   Most people start by putting a kettle on.

JENNY   No matter what I do, I always seem to forget just one thing. The bottles ... the bottles came from Willie, too. He invited me to an office party. Somebody asked if I was his girlfriend. How I laughed. Willie's girlfriend! But then it turned out *he'd* said I was. Poor Willie. We collected all the leftover drink and brought it here.

MOLLY   You musn't do that. Never let a man bring you back here after a party. You musn't let him in the door. Not even Willie.

JENNY   Something's got to happen sometime. *(Abruptly changing the subject)* I worked out the average ideal budget Duncan asked you for. How you spend your money.

MOLLY   He used to wonder how I spent my nights.

JENNY *(Producing extremely grubby sheet of paper)*
       On the basis of figures provided ...

MOLLY *(Taking it from her. Reading)* Coffee, cigarettes, cornflakes, sardines, pickles, soap and toothpaste. Each 12.5%. Total, one hundred.

JENNY I must have forgotten one important thing.

MOLLY It's fine, Jenny. I was just wondering about all these pickles.

JENNY Will you tell Duncan I worked it out? I'd like him to appreciate me.

MOLLY There's no mention of rent.

JENNY All you said was cornflakes.

MOLLY Nobody spends 12.5% of an income on soap and toothpaste.

JENNY Cross it out and put 'Maintenance'.

MOLLY What's that?

JENNY Governments have it.

MOLLY Give me a pencil. *(Crosses out)* I'll put it instead of pickles. What can I put for cornflakes?

JENNY Try 'Taxes', and for 'Cigarettes' you could have 'Savings'.

MOLLY Duncan may wonder about the sardines.

JENNY 'Health and Transportation.' 'Family Holidays' might be better than 'Soap and Toothpaste'.

MOLLY Coffee — do we leave coffee?

JENNY 'Children's Education.' What does that give?

MOLLY   Maintenance, Health and Transportation, Taxes, Savings, Family Holidays, Children's Education. Each, 12.5%. Total, one hundred.

JENNY   It's a good budget. Molly. It's serious. I mean that. A lot of people would be proud to have it.

MOLLY   My future. What I'm looking at is my future. Six multiplied by anything equals my future.

JENNY   We won't need budgets in our future. After victory we'll have whatever we require in the most ... in the most simple and natural way.

MOLLY   My money. He wants to know how I'm spending my money. Money *I* make.

JENNY   Actually, it's the first time I've ever made tea for anyone.

MOLLY   I've brought you a couple of muffins and the Lenin. You can keep 'What Is To Be Done?' as long as you like. If I ever feel I need it, I'll tell you.

JENNY   Thank you, Molly.

Too touched to say more. Puts muffins in toaster. Alarm bell. Yvonne Printemps.

TOASTER   The coast of Normandy was invaded by Allied forces early this morning. Prayers are being offered in thirty-seven parishes of this city for the success of the operation, the continued good health of Maréchal Pétain, and the total and entire destruction of the British fleet.

JENNY   It's here. It has happened. The change.

MOLLY   The great change.

JENNY   How will it be? Oh, tell me. The French workers were there, waiting for them?

MOLLY   With garlands of wildflowers.

JENNY   Don't tease. It's too serious. What happens now?

MOLLY   It depends on how and where the German workers might be waiting.

JENNY   Mrs. Bailey said ... and Willie always told us ...

MOLLY   Willie may have changed his mind.

JENNY   But we haven't, Molly. We haven't. Have we? The men won't put up with ... First thing they'll do is get rid of Franco ...

MOLLY   Get rid of us, you mean. Look, the muffins are burning. *(Pause)* I'm afraid of the change.

JENNY   *(Distracted. Alarmed)* It doesn't matter about the muffins. We can eat toast.

MOLLY   I wish the war could go on and on, forever, and that we could stay as we are. As we used to be. I wish we were sitting on Willie's front steps saying to each other, 'After the war'. 'After the war' — do you know what... it sounds like, now? A big, ugly, ramshackle new house no one had time to finish building. It will be a slum even before the paint dries.

JENNY   But we can build properly. That's what we said we were going to do.

MOLLY   What do you think is going to happen when all those men come back?

JENNY   They won't put up with Fascism. They won't take things lying down.

MOLLY   Oh, God, Jenny, this isn't instruction. Duncan reminds me in every letter that I'm holding *his* job. As for you, if you want to keep a foot in the door, stop pestering Mr. Gillespie. I'm telling you for your own good. Otherwise, you'll be out too. Out of the big, crumbling, decaying new house. Look at Willie. See how Willie moved in — he's deep in the safest part of it. The ground floor.

JENNY   That's not what you promised.

MOLLY   I promised you something out of books I couldn't even read. There, you can keep this. It's yours. *(Throwing pamphlet)* Revolution. Jenny's soft little revolution. Have you ever seen anyone killed? My father died in a bottle fight. Would you know how to hold a bottle? Would you know which end to break? *(Takes a bottle and breaks its neck)* Have you ever seen a knife fight? Do you know where to stick a knife? Cutting edge up? Down?

JENNY   Promise me what you promised.

MOLLY   *(Giving up)* All right. I promise.

JENNY   When? Soon?

MOLLY   Before next winter. And the first thing we'll do then is ...

JENNY   *(Happy)* ... get rid of Franco.

MOLLY   *(Making fresh tea)* The men will never put up with ...

JENNY   *(Putting bread in toaster)* ... a Fascist state. After what they've seen over there ...

MOLLY   ... they won't take things lying down.

Jenny (*Splashing white paint over SECOND FRON*) Contact with European workers ... (*No answer. Molly is trying to get English news*)

Jenny Wait, wait! You can't have toast and English news at the same time. The lights blow up.

Radio Because of the importance of today's events in Europe, the forty-ninth episode of 'Gordon and Carol Ann: A Marriage for Our Time' will not ... (*Explosion and blackout*)

SCENE VII

Summer 1944. Molly alone.

Large stack of blue airmail form letters. These should be larger than life, unfolding to a page about twelve inches square.

MOLLY   When Duncan left me and went overseas, the mails were in pretty bad shape, what with the submarines and the censors. So we decided to number our letters. That way, we thought we'd be able to read them in order, maintaining a steady, calm and coherent marital dialogue. Because it takes two to make a dialogue. In the right order. So far, Duncan has sent me 968 letters, to which I have responded with 970. I always try to keep one or two answers ahead. A wise marital precaution. Marriage is not only coherence and calm and order. It also requires foresight ... having a number of answers prepared before the other party has even thought of the questions. *(Takes top letter and unfolds it)* The first letter I sent Duncan was numbered 32. I said. 'Try and get close to the British working classes. Apparently they're no great stakes, dialectically speaking, but weak dialectic is better than no dialectic.' Duncan's answer was numbered 100: 'I hope that the day I come back I'll find you taking a shower, and that you won't hear me coming in, and that when I pull the shower curtain aside ...' I replied, letter number nine, 'The only place where pure Socialism seems likely to work is Czechoslovakia. My plan for the two of us is to go straight there after victory and help them build.' Duncan then wrote, 75. 'Or maybe we could take a hotel room for the first forty-eight hours ...' I responded with letter 664: 'We could make ourselves useful in Czechoslovakia. We could teach them basket-weaving.' He said, letter 32, 'Or maybe I could just ring the doorbell and you could come naked to the door.' My answer to that was, 'I wonder if they have birch trees in Czechoslovakia? We could teach them to make birch-bark sandals.' Duncan replied, number 517, 'Or maybe just once in the back of a car, like when we were engaged.' I next sent him letter number four: 'Try and get demobilized over there. I could join you and we could go straight to Czechoslovakia.' On which he wrote number 92: 'I dream about you. I've had you better and more often in dreams than in life.' To which I responded, 'I dream of a world burned down to its essential core of poets and philosophers.' Duncan said, letter 15, 'The advantage to all this dreaming is that if I'm killed I'll have had you the night before.' I answered, number three, 'Is it true about the girls there, that they can't get it enough?' He replied, 'Give my love to your mother.' I wrote, 'Learn some French in your spare time.'

He said, 'All my dreams are still sex, and still you,' I answered, 'You could do Czech Monday through

Wednesday, German on Thursday and Friday, Russian on Saturday and French on Sunday. Your Sundays sound dull.' He replied, 'They say you could stand on a chair and see all of Hamburg now. Nothing left more than a foot high.' I asked, 'But how can we export our hopes and dreams? And in what language?' Duncan answered, 'You should see the guys in my regiment cutting prisoners' throats. You'd think they'd been doing it all their lives.' I said, 'Did you get the Russian grammar I sent you? It was in a tin marked "Toffee."' He replied, 'They grab the prisoner and jerk his head back. Another guy shoves the knife in his throat.' I answered, letter 21: 'Is it true about the German girls, that they'll do it for ice-cream?' Duncan said, 'I've never knifed a prisoner myself, but I've watched them doing it.' I replied, 'Perhaps we could just live like sister and brother for a while when you come back.' He said, 'Or on the floor, with sunlight pouring in the window, and a bottle of cold white wine ...' I said, 'This isn't just leading up to revolution, Duncan; it is the revolution. Try and ...'

(She stops reading)

I dream, too. I dream every night and on Sunday morning. I've had Frank Sinatra in a dream. I've had Frank Sinatra, and Franklin D. Roosevelt, and Francis X. Bushman. He was a movie star. My mother used to think about Francis X. Bushman when she was making love with my father, so that if she had a boy he'd be like him. But she had me. I've had Stalin in a dream, and Tolstoy, and Trotsky, and Rasputin, and Kerensky, and the Tsar. I've had a drum major in the Black Watch. I've had the whole Eighth Army — that was quite a long dream, I've had John the Baptist, by a waterfall. I've had the Vicar of Wakefield. Gilbert and Sullivan. Pancho Villa. I've had a jockey, and I've had a horse. I've had the man who came to dinner and the man in the iron mask. I've had my mother's dentist. I've had Jack the Ripper, and Jack and Jill, and Jack the Giant Killer, and Jack-of-all-trades, and somebody called Jack Sullivan … I can't tell you much about Jack Sullivan. I never saw him again.

They all said, Molly. Molly, Molly, Molly.
I said, I'm here. I'm here.

But I've never had Duncan. Not once. Not once in a dream did I ever have Duncan. Never. Not ever. Not once.

SCENE VIII

December 1944.

Willie's new apartment.

Willie, Karl-Heinz.

Well-heeled bachelor lives here. Two long sleek sofas. Cocktails and cocktail shaker. Night. Snow outside window. Willie wears a bow-tie. Slight trace of former accent.

Karl-Heinz is Willie's age, about 29. Wears a dark pullover; remnants of unidentifiable uniform. To a North American, in 1944, he would seem bohemian, political, foreign and alarming. To a North American female eye, he would look doomed, unreal, a character in historical fiction neither rich nor poor, immensely puzzling.

KARL-HEINZ   All at once, I found myself in the street. On the other side of the barbed wire. Not a penny in my pocket. Wondering where I was going to sleep. But free. Free.

WILLIE   I just want to explain about my two friends before they arrive. Jenny and Molly ...

KARL-HEINZ   I owe you a great deal. The best friend I could ...

WILLIE   One of them is married. The other is ... or at least I think she is ... she seems so young. You see, in North America, the women ...

KARL-HEINZ   The internment camps don't compare with camps in Europe.

WILLIE   I wouldn't want you to make the European mistake of thinking the women mean what they seem to offer. They never quite know when they've made an offer, It's entirely innocent ... or ignorant...

KARL-HEINZ   I found camp life here a milder, duller experience.

WILLIE   Their whole training is ... to arouse interest. And that's it. That's all.

KARL-HEINZ   There was enough to eat, but all the food had the same taste and texture. Soft ... sweet ... like eating sugared cottonwool.

WILLIE   If you make the mistake of thinking they mean it ...

KARL-HEINZ   One of the guards asked if I'd ever seen a knife and a fork before ... if there were forks in Europe.

WILLIE   Kindness is mistaken for weakness here. Consideration makes them cruel. They expect love to be a fight for power.

KARL-HEINZ   The women must be something like sweet cottonwool, too.

WILLIE   If a man won't fight her, she buries him alive.

KARL-HEINZ   In all countries, the women are always exactly like the food. Take Switzerland, for instance ...

WILLIE   And yet, this hideous and unnatural system seems to have left them untouched. Even Molly seems ...
(A buzzer)
There they are. They're downstairs.

(Talks into housephone)
Molly? Jenny?

JENNY'S VOICE Willie. Dear Willie. It's so cold. Please let us in.

WILLIE   It was brave of you to come in a snowstorm.

JENNY'S VOICE Willie. Dear. Hurry up.

WILLIE   When I saw the snow. I wondered ...

MOLLY'S VOICE Will you just for God's sake press the god-damned buzzer and let us in? We're freezing our asses off down here.

Karl-Heinz stands. Willie opens door.

WILLIE   Here they are. Here's the lift. Hello, hello, hello, hello.

Jenny and Molly bundled in winter garments — leggings, boots, balaclava helmets, scarves, mittens. Hampered by clothing, they waddle in, shedding snow. Willie tries to introduce his friend.

MOLLY   *(Speaking only to Jenny)* Where do we undress?

JENNY   There's just the one room.

MOLLY   But what a room. He must be making a fortune now.

JENNY   The Picassos are reproductions. I think.

WILLIE   ... one of my oldest and closest friends ...

JENNY   *(To Molly)* Would you mind giving me a hand with my boots?

WILLIE   ... fought in Spain together ...

MOLLY   Christ ... I've forgotten our shoes.

JENNY   It's all right. I've got them.

WILLIE   ... was arrested by Franco's first cousin. Escaped. Crossed the Pyrenees ...

MOLLY   *(To Jenny)* I brought a curling iron. In case we need it.

Molly and Jenny take off scarves, mittens, boots, and coats. Shake off snow. Fold everything neatly on a sofa. Are now wearing cardigans, balaclava helmets, woollen leggings and woollen pants that extend from knee to waist.

JENNY   We should have brought some records.

MOLLY   What are all those records over there?

JENNY   A load of opera music. Nothing we can dance to.

Karl-Heinz moves off. Willie continues the introduction.

WILLIE   As he stood blindfolded before the firing squad, he had a remarkable experience, he heard a woman singing an Andalusian folk song ...

Molly and Jenny start to unbutton sweaters. Seeing that Willie is still there, they put their overcoats over their shoulder. With all possible modesty, remove sweaters, leggings and pants. Pants are rapidly slipped behind sofa cushion.

MOLLY   I should call my mother.

JENNY   She can see it's snowing. All she has to do is look out the window.

WILLIE   The song seemed to be telling him not to despair.

Finds himself trying to introduce someone who has disappeared. Gives up.

MOLLY   You can look now. He's gone.

JENNY   Did you ever see anything so sticky as poor Willie? He's like flypaper.

Molly and Jenny now wear short, pale dresses held up by minute shoulder straps. Pale silk stockings with seams. Matching shoes. Impression of fragility and near nudity. Pastel drawings on which men might leave fingermarks, if allowed too near. Still wearing balaclava helmets.

> JENNY   He has just the one Benny Goodman record. 'Memories of You' on one side and 'Avalon' on the other. He never plays it unless I'm here. Poor Willie. The thing is to make them keep playing 'Avalon'. The other side's too slow and it gives them a chance to … you know …

Molly and Jenny take off balaclava helmets. Hair upswept. They help each other with straggling ends, using rhinestone clips and slides. Carefully examine each other's makeup.

> KARL-HEINZ   *(To Willie)* Which is the married one?
>
> WILLIE   Later.
>
> KARL-HEINZ   I don't want a virgin. It's too much like forced labour.
>
> WILLIE   That's not why I invited them.
>
> KARL-HEINZ   This time last year I was wondering if I'd ever see a woman again.

Jenny and Molly engaged in rapid, solemn ritual — straightening stocking seams, adjusting garters, tugging girdles, fiddling with straps, peering down inside dresses as though making certain breasts are more or less in the right piece. Then, as if seeing Willie for the first time:

> MOLLY   Willie! Here we are!
>
> JENNY   Willie! Darling!

Immediately sit down, close together, at some distance from the men.

WILLIE (*Attempting host gambit*) I have ... presents for you. *(Two large oblongs of stiff cardboard)* Original advertising layouts. One for each of you. *(Molly and Jenny blank)* They ... they're mine. One is for talcum powder and the other ... for cream of celery soup.

JENNY *(Sincere)* Did you sign them?

WILLIE On the back.

JENNY Thank you, Willie. Thank you so much. It's the first time anyone's ever given me original art.

WILLIE Not Art. Artwork.

MOLLY I wouldn't mind having the soup.

JENNY Do they pay you money for making these? Do they pay you a lot? *(Looking around)* I guess they do. We always thought you were earning a great salary. But we thought you were being blackmailed. By the Trotskyites in Glasgow.

Willie completely silenced by this. Karl-Heinz takes over, pouring drinks, etc. Jenny and Molly clearly fascinated by Karl-Heinz.

JENNY Are you the one ... ?

MOLLY Willie mentioned?

KARL-HEINZ *(Fast)* ... good friend.

WILLIE ... best friend.

MOLLY ... longing to meet you.

WILLIE ... wanted to introduce him but ...

JENNY ... such fun ...

MOLLY   ... dying for a party ...

JENNY   Willie always has quantities of stuff to drink.

KARL-HEINZ   ... best friend ...

WILLIE   We're all best friends.

MOLLY   Keep your mind on the music.

JENNY   No, Willie ... 'Avalon'. We said 'Avalon'.

Karl-Heinz is here for the girls. The girls are here for a party. The men keep turning the record over to 'Memories of You' — Willie because it is all he can dance to, Karl-Heinz because it gives him a chance to hold on to Jenny or Molly.

'Avalon' too fast for the men. Jenny and Molly dance together. None of the pure high spirits of the polka in Scene III; rather, a tough sexual competition with Karl-Heinz as prize. Their first female rivalry.

Extreme tension.

Willie's unhappiness beyond simple jealousy. Molly and Jenny longing for something unexpected, overwhelming. At the same time, it would be inconceivable for either of them to take off so much as an earring. Karl-Heinz thinks they mean it. Lets them come to him. Which they do.

He appears to be confiding some secret to Jenny. Music stops. Karl-Heinz heard clearly:

KARL-HEINZ   And then I heard a girl's pure voice singing a Schubert lied, and I knew that somewhere outside the prison walls there was life ... sun ... women ...

Willie flings open window, admitting blast of wintry air.

JENNY   Willie ... we're freezing.

WILLIE   You can hardly see for smoke in here.

WHAT IS TO BE DONE?

MOLLY   Or outside for snow. How are Jenny and I ever going to get home?

Jenny shivers. Karl-Heinz moves closer still. Molly puts a sweater over her shoulders and joins Willie at the window. Noise of Saturday night in street: bawling, fighting, glass breaking, police whistles. Someone singing 'Bless 'em All' with this variation: 'There'll be no commotion/This side of the ocean/So cheer up, my lads …' etc.

MOLLY   Listen to them. That's all men are to Jenny and me. Voices in the street on Saturday night. Naturally, I don't mean you.

WILLIE   Or Mr. Gillespie.

MOLLY   Did Glasgow sound like this?

WILLIE   Sometimes.

MOLLY   Does it make you homesick?

WILLIE   No.

KARL-HEINZ   *(Stroking whichever part of Jenny he can get his hands on)* Women mean civilization.

JENNY   *(Struggling as with an octopus)* Some women are awful. There's one in my office … Miss Stribling … she stole my adding machine. And Miss Longhorn … you should see Miss Longhorn … she's so mean … so mean. She spilled ink on a beautiful … a beautiful graph I'd just made. 'The average age of cabinet ministers after 1923' … I never knew what Mr. Gillespie wanted that for …

Bundle sails in window. Willie slams window shut.

WILLIE   Don't touch it!

KARL-HEINZ   Get the women out of the room!

WILLIE   Yes ... you'd better go ... somewhere.

MOLLY   Where do you want us to go? You've seen the snow out there.

KARL-HEINZ   Get a pail of water.

JENNY   *(Picking up object)* It's just one of Mrs. Bailey's helmets. Look, Molly. It's quite long now.

MOLLY   Throw it back.

JENNY   No, it might hurt someone.

KARL-HEINZ   In prisons one receives such messages from the world outside. We were sixteen men, waiting to be shot ...

MOLLY   Mrs. Bailey knew we were here.

KARL-HEINZ   The message, no larger than a butterfly. 'Be brave', it said. No one knew which of us ...

JENNY   Mrs. Bailey always knows where we are. It's ... reassuring.

KARL-HEINZ   The Basque comrade was first to go, clenching his fist and crying something in his Stone Age tongue. Then ...

WILLIE   Why does it have to be Mrs. Bailey's? It could fit anyone.

KARL-HEINZ   It was the turn of Major Sharpe of British Intelligence. To the end, he pretended he was only an obscure camel driver. Discipline. Obedience. Impenetrable disguise. Not a word in English. Even when ...

JENNY   We have a perfect right to be here. We used to come to Willie for instruction.

KARL-HEINZ   Major Sharpe said goodbye to us in Aramaic. We sang 'Red Flag'.

MOLLY   She meant it as a joke.

WILLIE   Mrs. Bailey never jokes. *(Seems overcome)*

KARL-HEINZ   One of our guards ... a fresh-faced lad from an Armenian village ...

MOLLY   Willie's fainted.

JENNY   Sometimes he just goes to sleep.

KARL-HEINZ   Luckily, I could speak Armenian fluently. On the morning fixed for my execution, he brought me a complete Gay-Pay-Oo disguise ... the long overcoat ... the wide-brimmed felt hat ... the brown leather gloves ...
(Molly sleeps)

JENNY   Are you all right. Molly?

KARL-HEINZ   Suddenly I was in the street ... free ...

KARL-HEINZ   She's asleep.

KARL-HEINZ   Without a kopek in my pocket. But free. Free.
(Jenny sleeps)

KARL-HEINZ   I thought with a pang of the comrades left behind ... the Bulgarian ... the Belgian ... the Turk ... the ... the ...
(Sleeps)

Silence. Then sound from street, as of a new day — cars starting up, doorbells, a streetcar clanking. Colour of sky in window lightens from black to grey. Willie sits up. Covers Jenny tenderly with a coat. Goes out. The others waken one after the other.

MOLLY   I'd better call my mother.

KARL-HEINZ   Suddenly I realized it was April. I had forgotten that somewhere in the world April could still ...

JENNY   I'm hungry.

KARL-HEINZ   From an open window came the pure, sweet voice of a woman singing a Caucasian folksong.

JENNY   *(To Molly)* Is this still Spain?

MOLLY   It sounds more like ... Italy.

JENNY   One of those places
(Willie returns with coffee)

WILLIE   Karl-Heinz has been telling you about his escape from Lubyanka Prison.

MOLLY   Where's that?

WILLIE   In Moscow.

JENNY   In Moscow?

MOLLY   But there are no prisons in Moscow. Except ...

WILLIE   They were in a lesson I forgot... to teach.

MOLLY   *(Different tone)* There are no prisons ... except for ...

Molly and Jenny exchange a look. Instinctively clasp hands, as if denying last night's rivalry. Without a word, begin to put on their outdoor clothes, swiftly and efficiently handing each other garments as they disentangle them from the heap on the sofa. Karl-Heinz absorbed in his breakfast. Willie tries helplessly to interfere. Jenny and Molly talk to each other through him and around him.

WILLIE   I know what you think ... but it's wrong ...

MOLLY   Remember the old days at the Austro-Hungarian Friendship Club? How we drank.

JENNY   And danced.

WILLIE   Karl-Heinz is a brave, remarkable, loyal ...

MOLLY   We thought almost any foreigner had to be on our side.

JENNY   We never knew how to read the signs on the wall.

WILLIE   ... the most ignorant ... misunderstanding ... the most obstinate ... blind ... stupid ... cruel ...

JENNY   Except Trotskyites. We'd never met any.

MOLLY   Didn't even know what they looked like.

JENNY   Or Fascists. Had never even seen one.

WILLIE   It's my own fault, of course. I was the one who ...

MOLLY   It's hard for you, Jenny. Coming of age in a world without men. Just old men and foreigners and Trotskyites and leftovers. I was lucky to be two years older. I got married just in time.

JENNY   I appreciate the way you feel about me. Molly ... I'm sorry ... but you've got my pants on. *(They exchange)* Are the streetcars running?

MOLLY   I heard one.

JENNY   Mrs. Bailey was right.
(Willie gives up)

MOLLY   We should have listened to Mrs. Bailey.

Sidle to the door, as if afraid of being attacked. Jenny remembers her manners.

JENNY Thank you for the lovely party, Willie. We enjoyed ... quite a lot of it. Say ... say goodbye to your friend for us. Tell him ... no hard feelings. We don't quite know what to say to him. You see, he's our first Fascist.

Willie pours two stiff drinks and hands one to Karl-Heinz.

KARL-HEINZ *(After a moment)* What did she say?

WILLIE She said that you were her first.

KARL-HEINZ *(Pleased)* I thought so.
(Pause) Which one of the two was the virgin?

WILLIE Both.

Morning, Willie turns out lights.

KARL-HEINZ You don't know any more ... any other ...?

WILLIE No.

KARL-HEINZ Women ... in their minor, their subjective way ... are part of one's total political experience. No one was ever asked to take a vow of chastity. Except the Serbian partisans, I believe. But the Serbs ... the climate ...

WILLIE Some of us have chastity thrust upon us.

KARL-HEINZ ... darkness falling at three in the afternoon ... and the religion ... ikons glaring down on them ...

WILLIE Picasso can have the same effect.

KARL-HEINZ Women ... in their minor way ... are the yeast ... the leavening of political action.

WILLIE   Or a Spanish war poster, or a photograph of Stalin, I've never found the right picture.

KARL-HEINZ   Imagine Lenin without Krupskaya, Imagine ... *(Runs out of examples. (Willie picks up balaclava helmet and examines it)*

WILLIE   Karl-Heinz — when you write the long story of your political adventures, don't forget the wild night you spent in North America with the natural daughters of Bakunin and Queen Victoria. *(Opens window. Throws helmet out)*

SCENE IX

7 May 1945. Jenny's room.

Jenny and Molly.

A few changes; tablecloth over packing crate. A number of home-made lamps. Bookcase of planks and bricks. Lineup of bottles. SECOND FRON visible through white paint. Paintpots, phone, toaster and radio as they were. Picture of Mrs. Bailey's father replaced by Stalin. Meal of sorts laid out on crate. Wine.

Spring evening. Still light.

Molly wears a smart, tight suit and a hat with a veil. Long white gloves across her lap. Sits turned away from the table-crate; excessively off-hand; a model in Vogue *pretending to eat.*

Jenny reading a newspaper.

> JENNY *(Reading)* '... with an all-star cast including Franchot Tone, Clark Gable, Gary Cooper and Errol Flynn. Into the valley of the shadow, their hearts sang a tune.' Apparently it's about some awful thing that happens to a Red Cross nurse.
>
> MOLLY We've missed the beginning.
>
> JENNY No, just the newsreel. If we leave now we can still make the documentary. *(Reading)* 'How to Build an Igloo.'

MOLLY   I think I've seen it.

JENNY   (*Reading*) 'A full evening of thrilling entertainment. Free wartime peanuts. One Commando Crunch chocolate bar per person. Donald Duck, Pathé News, Documentary, two full-length features.'

MOLLY   What's the second feature?

JENNY   (*Reading*) '"Hearts Across the Desert" with Cary Grant, Robert Taylor and Mickey Rooney. Your heart will sing a tune.' That's all it says. There's a picture of them wearing solar topees. It must be about some awful thing that happens in a jungle.

MOLLY   I don't mind missing the one about the nurse. (*Pause*) Terrible noise in your street.

JENNY   I'm sorry.

MOLLY   What *are* they singing? If it *is* singing.

JENNY   'Roll Me Over in the Clover.'

MOLLY   Saturday night in Glasgow.

JENNY   Do you remember singing, 'We're marching with Chuuuuurchill ... ?'

MOLLY   Apparently Churchill has become a Fascist. So has de Gaulle. So has Roosevelt.

JENNY   Roosevelt, is dead.

MOLLY   Well, the new, then.

JENNY   The new one's a Fascist?

MOLLY   Out-and-out. Apparently.

JENNY   Stalin, too?

MOLLY   Stalin is waiting for the war to end so that he can enter a monastery. He was always a mystic. Essentially.

JENNY   Mrs. Bailey changed her mind about Stalin's picture. She said she'd rather have her father, after all. So we exchanged. *(Pause)* What does Duncan say?

MOLLY   About what?

JENNY   About all that.

MOLLY   Not much. How's Willie?

JENNY   I do not keep track of Willie. Willie means nothing to me.

MOLLY   Sorry.

JENNY   We always wanted a place where we could talk.

MOLLY   We are talking. We've talked about ...

JENNY   You said the thing about Glasgow.

MOLLY   And about Stalin. That was important.

JENNY   It certainly needed to be said.

Mrs. Bailey appears at window. Head and shoulders. Drops a very large bundle of knitted helmets on the floor.

JENNY   Mrs. Bailey! Won't you come in?

MRS. BAILEY   It's done. Finished.

JENNY   Your knitting is, Mrs. Bailey?

MRS. BAILEY   The war is over.

MOLLY   Over? Finished? Done with? Just like that?

MRS. BAILEY   Done and done and gone and gone: I'll have the picture, if you don't mind.

JENNY   Stalin, Mrs. Bailey? It's Stalin you want, after all?

MOLLY   She really ought to offer to trade. Next thing, she'll be trying to get her hands on the Royal Family.

MRS. BAILEY   You can have the balaclava helmets.

JENNY   All of them? Well ... thank you. Thank you very much.

Mrs. Bailey accepts Stalin and disappears.

JENNY   Do you suppose she really meant them for me? She finished just in time. In time for victory. *(Leaves bundle where it is)* We ought to ... I don't know ... do something.

MOLLY   Drink? *(Pours wine for both)*

JENNY   To ...

Neither can think of anything. Crash of breaking glass outside. Police siren. Ambulance bell.

JENNY   I wonder if Mr. Gillespie knows the war's over?

MOLLY   It could make a nice little story.

JENNY   I meant ... my impressions of the first hours of peace. 'A jubilant throng ...' Something like that.

Molly takes complete makeup equipment out of handbag — mascara, brush and comb, electric curling iron which she plugs into power point, lipstick, rouge, compact containing pancake makeup and sponge. Lifts veil. Examines face in mirror, inch by inch. No water to moisten sponge with. Considers wine. Wrong colour. Eye lights on gin. Uses that. Spits in mascara. Complete renovation. Examines face attentively. Satisfied. Lowers veil. Assumes Vogue pose again.

JENNY (*To Mr. Gillespie*) It's Jenny. Jenny, Mr. Gillespie. From ... yes, I imagine you do know where I'm from by now. The war is over, Mr. Gillespie. Over. Yes. The whole city is bursting with song. I thought you might like ... you might be able to use ... something. (*Song distinctly heard: 'Fuck 'em All'*)

JENNY They're singing their hearts out. Mr. Gillespie. It isn't what? That's terrible. What a terrible thing. Who could have made a mistake like that. And foisted it on the world. On a world longing for ... (*Fight just outside the window*)

JENNY And you ... you've brought out a special peace edition. All for nothing.
(*Street: 'So cheer up, my lads, fuck 'em all'*)

JENNY Well, would you like my impressions of the wrong victory? 'A misguided but joyous throng ...' No? I can't do anything for you at all? I see. I'm sorry. Goodnight, Mr. Gillespie.
(*To Molly*) The war isn't over. It won't be over until tomorrow. Somebody made a mistake. Mr. Gillespie says the noise around here is nothing. In some places, they're having real rioting and genuine looting.

MOLLY What if we had lost?

JENNY Lost the *war*?

MOLLY Would they still have been murdering one another in the street?

JENNY That's defeatist.

MOLLY Defeat and victory have no meaning now.

JENNY   They have until tomorrow. We still have a few hours left. A night. Tomorrow we'll have to change everything. The words we say. The things we mean. The things we want.

MOLLY   Barring accidents. Duncan survived. Tomorrow I'll be handed an I. O. U. God delivered the goods.

JENNY   *(Remembering)* You promised you would change. That you'd become whatever Duncan believed he married. You can't do it. It isn't possible.

MOLLY   A deal's a deal.

JENNY   Why couldn't your silly old peasant have done something as a favour? Just for once?

MOLLY   I wasn't asking a favour.

JENNY   Besides ... you may have changed. Without even trying.

MOLLY   I am exactly as I was when Duncan married me.

JENNY   How can Duncan remember, now, what he wanted all those years ago? He may have changed, too. You'll have to be introduced all over again.

MOLLY   '... And here's someone I'm sure you will enjoy meeting — your wife.'

JENNY   *Enchantée.*

MOLLY   *Monsieur.*

JENNY   *Madame.*

MOLLY   *La guerre vous a bien amusée, Monsieur?*

JENNY   *Énormément, Madame.*

MOLLY   *Et la paix?*

JENNY   He doesn't know yet. Be patient. Give him time.

MOLLY   In two years, he'll be thirty. He has survived a war. He has a son. He has survived both our fathers. If my father were here, tonight ...

JENNY   I never think that way. Oh, I did for a while. I tried. But I soon realized there was nothing but silence.

MOLLY   *(Change in tone)* 'Britain's finest hour,' my father would have said.

JENNY   I'll bet.

MOLLY   *(Cold)* After all ... once a sailor ...

JENNY   *(Trying to make sense of this)* Which navy was it, exactly?

MOLLY   Is there more than one? He was young when he left it. Impulsively. They begged him to stay. If he had, he would have been an admiral by now.

JENNY   He didn't want that, surely?

MOLLY   To each according to his needs.

JENNY   Nobody needs to be an admiral.

MOLLY   From each ...

JENNY   I just never pictured him as an admiral.

MOLLY   My father ran away from home because he wanted to become an admiral and his family didn't think it was good enough.

JENNY   Good enough for where?

MOLLY   For Cork.

JENNY   I believed ... or I imagined ...

MOLLY   After he left the Navy ... so impulsively ...

JENNY	Deserted, Molly. You always told me he'd deserted.
MOLLY	Came out here wearing the only clothes he owned.
JENNY	I remember that part.
MOLLY	He went to work for a major engineering firm. Manual labour. But they soon became aware of his quality. Moved him indoors. He learned drafting. The board of directors by a unanimous vote decided to send him to engineering school. He completed the four year course in one …
JENNY	But where, Molly? In a capitalist country?
MOLLY	Came back as chief of a branch office. Became vice-president … and acting general manager. By that time, his family back in Ireland had forgiven him. Just as he was about to come into his estate he died. Quite quickly. Death played a cruel game.
JENNY	*(Taking Lenin pamphlet from bookcase)* You won't be wanting this now.
MOLLY	The old what-are-we-supposed-to-be-doing? I believe it's a first edition. It must be worth something. *(Sees Jenny's face)* I didn't mean it. Though I don't see why I shouldn't mean it.

Jenny turns more lights on, breaking dark mood.

JENNY	Oh, Molly. Let's drink. Let's dance. Let's call everyone all over the world. Let's call the King of Egypt.
MOLLY	Who do we know in China?
JENNY	Call Stalin! Call the Pope! Call the Queen Mother!
MOLLY	Call Shostakovitch! Call Little Red Riding Hood!

JENNY *(Holding bottles up)* There's not more than an ounce in each, but if we put all the ounces end to end ...

MOLLY Let's call Franco.

JENNY Franco?

MOLLY Isn't that what we always said? First thing we do after victory is call Franco. Well, I know one call I do have to make, and that's to my mother.
(To her mother) Carina? *Ma sono io,* for God's sake. Stop crying. You've heard the news? How is Carlino? My son, Well, give it to him, but let him know at the same time that he's not to have it. Happy victory. *Ciao, Bella!*

JENNY What will Mrs. Bailey do now? Will she go underground, do you think?

No answer. Molly dances around waving a glass and frying pan.

MOLLY Let's drink all the drink! Let's burn all the toast! Let's fry all the eggs!

Jenny flings the bundle of helmets in the air. Begins to pull a strand of bright wool, turning it around the furniture.

MOLLY Be careful. It's unravelling.

Wild dance continues to the sound of drunken singing in the street.
Laughter.
Gradual darkness.

RADIO *(In the dark)*
(Singsong, emphatic, endlessly cheerful)
That's it, folks. A false alarm. The war's still on. The Prime Minister has issued a statement. I quote:

'For the sake of those citizens of freedom-loving countries who crave continuity, the war has been prolonged until tomorrow'. Remember, there are only a few hours left to buy Victory Bonds. Don't miss your last chance for a foolproof, can't-fail investment.

Last strains of 'A-Hunting We Will Go'.
Slow. A melancholy note.
A dying fall.
Darkness and silence.

SCENE X

8 May 1945. Jenny's room. Broad daylight sun. The unravelled wool like a bright haystack, with the telephone buried inside. On the wall:

V ie
  ictoire
  érité

Jenny prone on the floor, sleeping. Shoes off, hair undone. Silence. Then child is heard, bouncing a ball:

    CHILD   Cain and Abel
                 Married Betty Grable;
                 They lived in a storie
                 With Clark Gable.

Gradually rising, the sound of official victory: church bells; booming of cannons; 'Pomp and Circumstance', taken very slow; cadence of a victory speech — simply the cadence, the drone, without the words.

Jenny stirs, gets to her knees, pushes her hair away from her face. Crawls on all fours to the radio and turns it on. The words of the speech outside come in plain:

    RADIO   And I say to you, as I said to the voters of this
                 district, when it seemed that our darkest hour ...

Jenny turns it off. Shakes the bread wrapper, but no bread, and so no French news. Crawling over to the heap of wool, burrows inside, and drags out the telephone, which she dials with some fumbling and difficulty, muttering all the while.

JENNY *(Trouble speaking. At first slightly hoarse)* It's Jenny here. Jenny. Molly's friend. I'm not trying to disguise my voice, Mrs. McCormack. It's just that you're the first person I've talked to this morning — this afternoon, then. Could I speak to Molly? Why, is she still sleeping? She's taken her son to the victory parade? Molly has? I see.

I'm sorry. Mrs. McCormack, it just never occurred to *me* that I was a bad influence on Molly. Well, of course, I can see that you might see it that way, but … Look, Mrs. McCormack. I'm afraid I've got to hang up. I'm dreadfully sick. I don't know what the matter is. It feels like sunstroke combined with food poisoning.

I think I'm dying. Really, I think so. It's what? Hangover? I thought only men got that. You could be right. I'm twenty-one. I suppose there isn't much I can still do with impunity. Do with … not much I can still get away with. Drink water. All right. I'll do that. Drink water, and water and water. Water. Water. Drink water, and don't call Molly. Molly's a married … she's a what? She's a married lady. Lady. Married lady. I'm not laughing, Mrs. McCormack. I'm too sick to laugh. I'm trying to remember what you just said. Drink water, and don't call Molly. Thank you for the advice about the water.

Happy what? Happy Victory Day? Same to you. Nice to see things normal again? Yes. Yes. Goodbye, Mrs. McCormack. Say goodbye to Molly.

Gets to her feet. Takes a moment to steady. Tries to pick up the heap of wool but has no idea what to do with it.

The polka she and Molly danced to in Scene III starts loudly and suddenly and stops with the same suddenness. Jenny indicates the V painted on the wall.

JENNY   Molly and I painted that last night. Sometime during the final hours. The final hours of the old way of life, gone forevermore. We're some hours into the new era. It doesn't feel too steady. It will take time to get used to peace … and justice … and …

Molly painted the V. It's a bit crooked. I wrote the words. They're in French because I couldn't remember anything good in English starting with V. Apart from Victory.

We never had the right language.

I said to Molly, 'It will be a clean new world, with a clean swept sky.'

Molly said, 'No, I see it more like a big old kitchen, with everyone crowded and comfortable, and enough tea and bread-and-butter to go round.'
The first thing they'll do now is get rid of Franco. I suppose. I mean, the men will never put up with … but first of all, there will have to be elections. Everywhere. Spanish elections, Greek elections. Polish elections, French elections, Lithuanian elections. Austro-Hungarian … no, that's wrong.

The men will never put up with a Fascist state. They've learned something over there.

Contact with other workers. Won't take things lying down anymore. The way they took ... It's just a question of ...

Mr. Gillespie said, 'Show me a reasonable Socialist and I'll show you a reasonable Capitalist'. It doesn't work if you say it the other way. I don't know why. 'Show me a reasonable Capitalist and I'll show you ...' It doesn't work.

My mother was here. She called me at the office. She said, 'Come and have tea with me. I'm at the Ritz-Carlton.' She said, 'What do you mean, you can't? I always had time for *my* mother.' She said, 'If that's the case, why don't you quit your job and just get married?' She said, 'You're talking rubbish. It's just as easy to love a rich man as a poor one. It doesn't take any more effort.'

I loved Willie. I really did. Even after Mrs. Bailey said he wasn't useful.

Willie's instruction.

'March 1848 Revolution. Led to some deaths. In Berlin, 187 dead, known as the *Märzgefallen*. Probably because they fell in March.'

Willie's instruction.

When it finally happened, I said to him, 'Is that all?' I said, 'You mean that was it?' I said, 'Are you sure there isn't some other thing we can do?' After all that wondering and trying to read the last paragraph of Duncan's letters.

I said. 'Are you *sure* that was it?'

I could have worked out the overage for something like that in a minute. But I didn't say so. I just asked, 'Is that all?' politely. Molly and I never read 'What Is To Be Done' We never had the right language. I read some other things. In English. Like 'The Role of Women in Revolution.' Actually, it isn't all that great a role. When he jumps out of the airplane, you hang around in a cornfield waiting to carry the parachute.

I read 'The Rime of the Ancient Mariner.' 'Ode to a Grecian Urn.' In English.

Molly used to recite a poem called 'Comrade.' She recited the whole thing one time when we were sitting on Willie's front steps. I said, 'I shall remember it forever.'

It went, 'Something and something, and ... and ... And still I answer the salutation proudly.' Or else it went, 'And *yet* I answer the salutation proudly.'

I've forgotten. I've already forgotten. It's gone.

I used to recite 'The Death of Minnehaha.' 'In the snow a grave they made her.'

No, before that. Wait. Before that. Two pages before. Well, she dies, you see, and *he* says ... '"Farewell!" said he, "Minnehaha!"'

No, before that. About a page before. 'And he rushed into the wigwam.'

No, before that.

'Rushed the maddened Hiawatha, Wrapped in furs and armed for hunting.'

Before or after? Before, before.

'The maddened Hiawatha.' She must have been dead. The snowstorm came first, then he rushed into the wigwam. Wait. Wait.

'Ever deeper, deeper, deeper, Fell the snow o'er all the landscape.'

It was before.

'Oh, the wasting of the famine! Oh, the blasting of the fever!'

'Farewell' should come after that. About four pages after. She dies in the middle of a page, right-hand side, '"Farewell!" said he,' What did she say? Wait. Wasted and blasted, blasted and wasted.

She said ... I don't know. I don't know. I don't think she said anything.

Room darker and darker.

Mr. Gillespie said, 'What the coming generation needs is an iron hand.' An iron hand. Mr. Gillespie? It's Jenny here, from Appraisements and Averages. This is our first day ... the first day of the new era. I thought you'd like a nice little story to celebrate. Remember the series we ran? Towards a Better World? We're in it. A whole day in. Almost. So. Towards a Better World. There's a place here where they lock girls up and work them to death. Really, to death. They're locked up and they die.

No, not a ... not one of those. It's a laundry. A place where people send their washing. The girls are called 'delinquent Catholics.' Delinquent Catholics. A delinquent Catholic is a girl who's been raped by a member of her family. For a Protestant to be a delinquent she has to be raped by a total stranger. Like, someone in a railway station. Someone who doesn't know her name. But with the Catholic girls, well, it's mother's sister's husband, father's nephew's brother, cousin's son's son. That's what counts. These girls ... they're never seen again. Mr. Gillespie. Their heads are shaved. They're starved for food and starved for sleep, and they have a cruel punishment, and they work in the laundry, and they die. The place is a stone house behind a wall. You must have gone by the wall a thousand times.

Your wife sends her tablecloths there? Not all the tablecloths. Only one. Well. I can imagine that if you have St. Ursula and the Thousand Virgin Martyrs embroidered on a tablecloth ... Done in network? Done in network. I imagine if you've got St. Ursula and the Thousand ... Not all the virgins, just some of the heads? If you've got... a tablecloth with St. Ursula and some of the Thousand Virgin Martyrs' heads done in network, you don't want just any old laundry ...

It must be beautiful. I agree. I agree.

But these girls.

A way of cleansing society?

I don't think it's a very good way. Not that I mean to contradict you. I don't know why society needs to be cleansed at all. It just needs to be ... a bit more curious.

Learning a useful ... but what does it matter if they learn something useful? I'm not arguing. I'm not saying your wife's tablecloth isn't a work of art. A museum piece, I'm sure it *is* a museum piece.

I'm only saying that I don't see why a girl who's been raped by her sister's husband's father's cousin has to wash, starch and iron St. Ursula and the Thousand Virgin Martyrs in order to cleanse society.

I'm not being offensive ... I wouldn't dream ... it's not my ... I'm not like ... I'm sorry, Mr. Gillespie. I certainly didn't mean to upset you. Not now, at the beginning of the new ... on Day One of the new ... I thought it might be good to settle one or two unfinished matters from the old era, The old era. Because of course it will be different now. I'm sorry, I truly am. The *last* thing I ever mean to do is upset anyone. I can see that you're upset. I've been disturbing you, taking your mind off—

... You're right. It is a new world. Down to brass tacks. Two and two make. Shoulder to the. A lot to be done. Problems facing. Yes. If people minded their own business, we'd all be a lot.

Appraisements and Averages to be expanded.

Good future for me if I'll only.

A new retirement plan.

New desk. New lights, to spare my eyesight. New calculating machine. For me. For *me?* In no time I could rise to. Climb to—

Become assistant to—

Have all remarked on how bright I am.

New holidays. One week without pay for four years, then one week with pay and one without for six years, then two weeks with pay and one without for three years, then.

If only I can keep to the straight. My eye on the. My nose to the. My mind on. A time for life and a time for dreams. Yes, I can see that.

I'm sorry, Mr. Gillespie. I'm sorry I started the new era off by worrying you. Spoiled one of the best days of your. It won't happen again. Yes, that's a promise. It will never happen again.

Yes, like a good girl.

It won't happen again.

It won't happen again.

The voices of Jenny and Molly are heard, from Scene V, sweetly singing 'The Internationale.'